Dickens at Doug

JOHN GREAVES

*Dickens
at
Doughty Street*

ELM TREE BOOKS
HAMISH HAMILTON · LONDON

First published in Great Britain 1975
by Elm Tree Books Limited
90 Great Russell Street, London, WC1
Copyright © 1975 by John Greaves
SBN 241 89197 3

Printed in Great Britain
by Ebenezer Baylis & Son Ltd
The Trinity Press, Worcester, and London

CONTENTS

LIST OF ILLUSTRATIONS

FOREWORD

In all the thousands of books that have been written about every aspect of the life and work of Charles Dickens, no one has yet recounted the period that he spent at the charming terrace house at 48 Doughty Street in Bloomsbury.

Since it has been for half a century the London Dickens Museum, and also the headquarters of the Dickens Fellowship, the author is the natural choice to chronicle the three years of Dickens's life there with his young family.

John Greaves, who claims to have been weaned on Charles Dickens in the days before strained baby foods, has devoted all his life to the study of Dickens, and at least a third of it to his invaluable work as Secretary to the Fellowship.

Priestley, Angus Wilson, Humphrey House, Margaret Lane, the Hardwicks—the literary world still abounds with fond and famous chroniclers. But I venture to say that there is only one person who can give you the answer to the most esoteric question about the least important character in the least known story, *without looking it up*.

Just as, at Mr Spenlow's dinner, Dora was food and drink to David Copperfield, John Greaves is soaked and nourished in the works of Charles Dickens. He carries about with him a nineteenth century aura of honest kind manners. Quotations spring from his lips as easily as clichés from the rest of us.

Somebody once said, 'There is a tiny bit of Dickens in all of us', meaning that there is no one alive who could not relate intensely and personally to at least something Dickens wrote. In John Greaves, there is a healthy chunk of Dickens.

Apart from his books and work with the Fellowship, the chunk has manifested itself mostly in the 2,000 lecture recitals he has given to audiences all over the world. From his first appearance at fourteen as Scrooge before a captive family audience, through Fagin in a green limelighted cell for the edification of First War troops, he arrived at his present format, which uses no make-up or costume. The words

7

of Dickens create pictures in the mind. John's exuberant voice and face materialise them for the eye and ear.

He is often accused of looking like Mr Pickwick. But isn't it the other way round? Not so much that a live human being is like a character in a book, but that the characters in Dickens's books are like live human beings. If he is to be stuck with the Pickwick image, why not say that Mr Pickwick is like John Greaves?

To those who have visited the Museum at 48 Doughty Street, this book will add extra value and interest to the initiation given by the priestesses who emerge beaming from the back room to show you, 'This is where the mutton was carved . . . this is where Mary Hogarth died . . .', as enthusiastically as if you were the first visitor, instead of the millionth.

Here, where Dickens lived from 1837 to 1839, *Pickwick* and *Oliver Twist* were finished, *Nickleby* was written, and *Barnaby Rudge* begun. Here Dickens was shocked for life by the tragic death of his young sister-in-law, which was to doom Little Nell to her untimely deathbed. Here, in the kitchen, swept and sniffled the tweenies from the local orphanage who gave birth to the Marchioness.

Here Mamie and Katey were born. Here Charles Dickens, still happy in his marriage, and mountingly sure and successful in his work, first began to taste what it was going to be like to be the most famous man in the world.

MONICA DICKENS

Introduction and acknowledgments

At the Sixteenth Annual Conference of the Dickens Fellowship at Cheltenham, in May 1922, Mr B. W. Matz, the Society's founder and Hon. Editor of *The Dickensian*, put forward the suggestion that the Fellowship should mark its coming of age by purchasing 48 Doughty Street, and preserve it as a National Dickens Library and Museum. The property, plans for the destruction of which were far advanced, was secured by Messrs Matz, Dexter and Green.

In his Presidential speech at Caxton Hall, in October 1922, Sir Frederick Macmillan inaugurated the raising of a Fund by which the Fellowship could take over the property. It is interesting to note that Sir Frederick also mentioned on that occasion that he was fortunate in having actually heard Dickens give his farewell reading in St James's Hall, London, in March 1870.

The Fund was raised by efforts of members of the Fellowship and as a result of National appeals. After protracted negotiations the property was taken over by the Fellowship and registered in perpetuity with the Official Trustee of Charity Lands. It was opened to the public by Lord Birkenhead on 9 June 1925 and is governed by a Board of Trustees consisting of seven members of the Dickens Fellowship and one representative each of the City Corporation, the Greater London Council and the Camden Council.

The aim of the book has been to present a reasonably complete account of the life of Dickens during his occupation of 48 Doughty Street and his extraordinary rise to fame in that short time against rather difficult odds.

I greatly appreciate the privilege accorded to me by the Trustees of the Dickens House in accepting this book to mark the Fiftieth Anniversary of the opening of the Museum to the public and for permission to use illustrative material from its unique library collection. I would like to record my acknowledgment and thanks to the Clarendon Oxford Press for kind permission to quote from the Pilgrim Edition of *The Letters of Charles Dickens* and also to the Nonesuch

Press. My sincere thanks to those good friends who have been so helpful in typing, reading and checking the script and for tendering most useful suggestions for amendments —Priscilla Foot and Jackie Whiting, and to members of the staff at Doughty Street, in particular to Marjorie Pillers, Curator of the Dickens House, for her invaluable help in selecting and arranging the illustrations. But for these good people I would have found it difficult to keep to a deadline to ensure publication on the relevant date, to mark the fiftieth anniversary of the opening of the House to the public, and which is now attracting over 30,000 visitors every year from all over the world.

JOHN GREAVES

CHAPTER 1

'Room to swing a cat'

'You know Trotwood, I don't want to swing a cat. I never do swing a cat.'[1] That was Mr Dick's plaintive remark to David Copperfield, when David's landlady, Mrs Crupp, indignantly assured him that in the alternative accommodation being offered to him—a room over a chandler's shop in Hungerford Market—there wasn't room to swing a cat.

Although Dickens himself hardly wished for room to swing a cat when contemplating a move from Furnival's Inn, not having acquired any pets at that time, he certainly did need more living accommodation.

Before his marriage to Catherine Hogarth, Dickens had moved from his bachelor quarters at 13 Furnival's Inn and taken a three-year lease of No. 15, from Christmas 1835, although he did not move until the middle of February 1836. Here he enjoyed three third-floor rooms, a basement kitchen, a cellar, and a lumber room on the top floor. The lease of 13 Furnival's Inn contained the clause:

> And further, the said Charles Dickens shall not and will not at any time during the continuance of the Tenancy permit or suffer any Children to reside or live in the said Chambers ...

Although the lease of No. 15 Furnival's Inn does not appear to be with the other papers at the Dickens House it is natural to expect that the same conditions must have applied. The arrival of a son—Charles Culliford Boz, on 6 January 1837, may have been another reason for contemplating a move, as well as the necessity for more space, with his fifteen-year-old brother Fred, and his sister-in-law, Mary Hogarth to accommodate besides his wife and himself; and so he began to search for a house.

Except for a few minor items there are no indications in his letters of the furniture he had at Furnival's Inn, or what extra items he bought on the occasion of his marriage (2 April 1836). No doubt his purchases were fairly modest, as he could not afford much at that time. It seems that he must have had a piano, because when he came to write his operetta, *The Village Coquettes*, John Hullah, the composer, tried out the music in Furnival's Inn. Maybe it was the family piano from his parents broken up home in Bentinck Street. One letter to his bride-to-be mentions some trifling purchases—a pair of quart decanters, and a pair of pints, a crystal jug, and three brown jugs with plated tops, for beer and hot water, a pair of lustres and two magnificent china jars—all of which he considered were bargains.[2]

In *Martin Chuzzlewit*, John Westlock lived in Furnival's Inn, High Holborn:

> There are snug chambers in those Inns where the bachelors live, and, for the desolate fellows they pretend to be, it is quite surprising how well they get on. John was very pathetic on the subject of his dreary life, and the deplorable makeshifts and apologetic contrivances it involved; but he really seemed to make himself pretty comfortable. His rooms were the perfection of neatness and convenience at any rate ... suddenly there appeared a being in a white waistcoat, carrying under his arm a napkin, and attended by another being with an oblong box upon his head, from which a banquet, piping hot, was taken out and set upon the table.
>
> Salmon, lamb, peas, innocent young potatoes, a cool salad, sliced cucumber, a tender duckling, and a tart—all there. They all came at the right time ... He was never surprised, this man; he never seemed to wonder at the extraordinary things he found in the box; but he took them out with a face expressive of a steady purpose and impenetrable character, and put them on the table ... dinner being done, and wine and fruit arranged upon the board, he vanished, box and all, like something that had never been.[3]

But John Westlock assured Ruth Pinch that normally he was dull and solitary: 'It was a wretched life, he said, a miserable life. He thought of getting rid of the chambers as soon as possible.' Dickens was still thinking of those chambers in Furnival's Inn when writing *Martin Chuzzlewit*, six years after leaving them.

The bachelor gadgets he knew from his various lodgings seem to have intrigued Dickens, to judge by his description of Dick Swiveller rousing the Single Gentleman lodger in the story, *The Old Curiosity Shop*.

> The lodger took from his great trunk, a kind of temple, shining as of polished silver, and placed it carefully on the table . . .
>
> Into one little chamber of this temple, he dropped an egg; into another some coffee; into a third a compact piece of raw steak from a neat tin case; into a fourth he poured some water. Then, with the aid of a phosphorous-box and some matches, he produced a light and applied it to a spirit-lamp which had a place of its own below the temple; then he shut down the lids of all the little chambers; then he opened them; and then, by some wonderful and unseen agency, the steak was done, the egg was boiled, the coffee was accurately prepared, and his breakfast was ready.[4]

One wonders whether Dickens had something like this in his bachelor chambers in Furnival's Inn, or had seen one elsewhere. However, for a young man setting up a family home in 1837, a wife and sister-in-law and a younger brother to run errands were a decided improvement, though perhaps more expensive luxuries.

He wrote about chambers in other books—in *Pickwick Papers* ('The Old Man's Queer Client') and later in *Great Expectations*. One paper called 'Chambers', contributed to *All The Year Round* in 1860, was devoted entirely to the subject. Dickens referred to these places as being queer and lonely and subject to somewhat ghostly events. He mentioned many others—Gray's Inn, Lyons Inn, New Inn, Staple Inn, Barnard's Inn, Clement's Inn, Clifford's Inn, Lincoln's Inn and the Temple. His other references to Furnival's Inn were in his first and last books—*Sketches by Boz* and *The Mystery of Edwin Drood*.

In 'The Bloomsbury Christening', contributed in 1834 to *The Monthly Magazine*, and later included in the collection *Sketches by Boz*, it was outside Furnival's Inn that Nicodemus Dumps was robbed of the silver christening mug he had bought for his godson, Master Frederick Charles William Kitterbell.

In *The Mystery of Edwin Drood*, when Rosa Bud flees from Cloisterham to escape from the unwelcome attentions of John Jasper, she goes to her guardian in London, who lives in chambers in Staple Inn. Faced with the unexpected necessity of finding temporary accommodation for his ward for the night, Mr Grewgious takes a room for her in Furnival's Inn, across Holborn. Dickens describes Rosa's room as 'airy, clean, comfortable, almost gay',[5] so thirty-four years after leaving, he still had pleasant recollections of Furnival's. Maybe, in putting the dainty and beautiful Rosa Bud there, he still thought of Mary Hogarth in the same setting.

It was the hotel in Furnival's Inn, however, that earlier in the same story had the honour of providing the dinner for Mr Grewgious and his guests, at which two waiters attended—an immovable waiter and a flying one:

> The flying waiter who had brought everything on his shoulders, laid the cloth with amazing rapidity and dexterity; while the immovable waiter, who had brought nothing, found fault with him. The flying waiter then highly polished all the glasses he had brought, and the immovable waiter looked through them. The flying waiter then flew across Holborn for the soup, and flew back again, and then took another flight for the joint and poultry, and flew back again, and between whiles took supplementary flights for a great variety of articles, as it was discovered from time to time that the immovable waiter had forgotten them all. But let the flying waiter cleave the air as he might, he was always reproached on his return by the immovable waiter for bringing fog with him, and being out of breath. At the conclusion of the repast, by which time the flying waiter was severely blown, the immovable waiter gathered up the tablecloth under his arm with a grand air, and having sternly (not to say with indignation) looked on at the flying waiter while he set the clean glasses round directed a valedictory glance towards Mr Grewgious, conveying: 'Let it be clearly understood between us that the reward is mine; and that Nil is the claim of this slave,' and pushed the flying waiter before him out of the room.[6]

About ten months before their move to Doughty Street, Mary Hogarth, Dickens's sister-in-law, wrote to her cousin after staying with the Dickenses at Furnival's Inn:

> I have just returned home from spending a most delightfully happy month with dearest Catherine in her own house. I only wish you could see her in it, and sincerely hope you may some day or other, not far distant, she makes a most capital housekeeper and is as happy as the day is long—I think they are more devoted than ever since their marriage if that be possible—I am sure you would be delighted with him if you

knew him he is such a nice creature and so clever he is courted and made
up to by all the literary Gentlemen, and has more to do in that way
than he can well manage.[7]

From this letter, it seems that the young couple were
very happy, and it is quite obvious that Mary Hogarth
thought very highly of her brother-in-law.

This letter, one of only two from Mary Hogarth
known to exist, and now on exhibition in the Dickens
House Museum, in Mary's bedroom, is written, it will
be noticed, in both directions on the same sheet of
paper, so that the lines crossed. This was customary with
longer letters in those days, when paper and postage was
very expensive. Even early in this century the custom
survived, and I remember an aunt of mine writing her
letters in both directions. It did make their reading a little
difficult, but it was quite possible with fairly clear and bold
handwriting.

In addition to earning 5 guineas a week from journalism,
plus an additional 2 guineas for short stories contributed
to the paper, Dickens was receiving a further steady
income for the writing of *Pickwick Papers*, and dearer
accommodation could therefore be contemplated.

The house agents and upholsterers, Messrs Thomas
Handisyde & Son of 55 Lamb's Conduit Street were
instructed accordingly,[8] and Dickens accompanied by Mary
went round viewing properties, while Kate stayed at home
with the baby Charles. When this son had been born and
Kate's mother and Dickens's mother had moved in, there
was no room for Mary, and Dickens had to take her back
at night to her parents' home at Brompton.[9]

It was on 4 February 1837 that Dickens and his wife
went again to Mrs Nash's cottage at Chalk, near Gravesend
in Kent, where they had spent their honeymoon. (This was
not the cottage now marked with a plaque, but one further
along the village street, which was demolished some years
ago.) A few days later Dickens returned to London by
steamer, on business, but being delayed at Bentley's, the
publisher's office, and taking time to view a house, he
missed the steamer and had to return by the Dover coach.[10]

Just over a month later, in a letter dated March 1837,
Thomas Handisyde wrote to Edward Wilson Banks, a

solicitor of Witham, Essex, whose father, the Rev. Joseph
Staines Banks, a vicar of Hemingford Grey, Hants., was
owner of the property, to the effect that Mr Dickens was
wishing to treat for 48 Doughty Street on a three-year
agreement at £80 per annum, and that he was agreeable
to painting the front drawing-room and blind frames round
the window. Attention was also drawn to a ceiling that
needed cleaning. Mr Dickens, advised the letter, required
an early answer at either 30 Upper Norton Street (presumably John Dickens's address at that time) or at 75 [sic]
Furnival's Inn, for he had to make a choice out of the houses
he had seen.

The estate agent's letter is interesting because of the
mistakes in it, which cannot be attributed to a typist, for
the letter was handwritten. First there is a reference to Mr
Dickens editor of the *Picnic,* later to Mr Wickens, and
finally to Mr D, proprietor of the *Pickwick* and known by
the name of Boz. His address was also wrongly given as
75 Furnival's Inn. Dickens was certainly not well known
at that time, though he became so very soon afterwards.

The Rev. Banks agreed to the terms and a three-year
lease of the premises was granted on 3 April 1837. Dickens
obtained an advance of £100 from Bentley against his
contract to write a novel, to cover the expenses of the move.
The rental for the twelve-roomed house of £80 per annum
was a substantial increase on the £50 yearly rental hitherto
paid for the chambers at 15 Furnival's Inn. The lease on
these premises was not due to expire until 25 December
1838, and although Dickens tried to sub-let the chambers,
he was unsuccessful and therefore had to pay the double
rent for eighteen months. The move to Doughty Street
probably took place during the end of March and beginning
of April.[11]

The agent's letter and the lease of 48 Doughty Street can
be seen at the Dickens House Museum. Dickens finally
terminated his lease of the Furnival's Inn premises in a letter
to Thos. Grissell, Samuel Morton Peto and Edward
Gardner, the termination taking effect on 25 December
1838.[12]

It may be interesting to trace briefly the history of 48
Doughty Street prior to Dickens occupying the premises.

At Michaelmas 1799, Elizabeth Doughty granted a lease to John Wilson, architect, of No. 38 (later 48) Doughty Street. At that time, the property was quite an extensive one, stretching 70 feet eastward from Doughty Street, and a non-residential part, extending a further 63 feet eastward and 120 feet southward. It comprised a large plot of land extending behind several houses in Doughty Street, which is now covered by the buildings in Brownlow Mews. In 1822, the occupant was Henry Jackson, who let the property to William Greenfield for fourteen years, at a rental of £105 per annum. By this time the property was owned by the Rev. Joseph Staines Banks, whose business affairs were dealt with by his son, Edward Wilson Banks.

According to the schedule with the lease, the top floor contained two 'garretts' with various fittings. On the second floor was a front room (which became the bedroom of Dickens and Kate), a dressing-room and a back room with cupboards (Mary Hogarth's bedroom). Fred probably slept in one of the top floor rooms or 'garretts' as they were called, and the other was possibly occupied by the nursemaid and the baby and later babies or maybe other domestic servants. It seems possible that when Mary died Fred may have been moved into her room. The first-floor front room became the drawing-room, and the small back room the novelist's study. On the first landing, between the first and ground floors was a toilet, but of course no bathroom. All the water for baths had to be heated in the basement and carried up to the bedrooms in cans by the servants. The ground floor contained a front room and back parlour—the dining-room in the front and the morning room behind, the latter overlooking the small garden. At the end of the passage from the front door was a cloakroom leading into the garden—now extended to form the Museum shop. The extent of this small cloakroom, immediately below the toilet above can be easily traced today by the ridge along the shop ceiling and was undoubtedly used for visitors' hats and coats, and also for the baby's pram. The basement contained a front and back kitchen and a wash-house with a copper and sink, both of which are there today and on view. There was a coal cellar under the pavement, gained through the area, and a wine cellar under the garden, and a basement toilet.[13] Only the front basement kitchen has been substantially altered since Dickens occupied the premises. This has been converted into an Elizabethan kitchen, similar to that at Manor Farm, Dingley Dell, in *Pickwick Papers*. The whole house was of course lighted by candles or oil lamps.

It is strange that Dickens should have unconsciously anticipated the number of the house in which he was to live. In May 1834, he wrote a two-part story called 'The Boarding House', which was published in *The Monthly Magazine* and later in the collection known as *Sketches by Boz*. He was living at that time with his parents at 18 Bentinck Street. In this story—long before he could have known anything about 48 Doughty Street, the following appears:

> 'God bless me!' exclaimed Tomkins, who had been looking out at the window. 'Here—Wisbottle—pray come here—make haste.' Mr Wisbottle started from the table, and everyone looked up. 'Do you see,' said the connoisseur, placing Wisbottle in the right position—'a little more that way: there—do you see how splendidly the light falls upon the left side of that broken chimney-pot at No. 48?' 'Dear me! I see,' replied Wisbottle in a tone of admiration. 'I never saw an object stand out so beautifully against the clear sky in my life,' ejaculated Alfred ... 'I have frequently observed a chimney-pot in College Green, Dublin, which has a much better effect,' said the patriotic O'Bleary, who never allowed Ireland to be out done on any point. The assertion was received with obvious incredulity for Mr Tomkins declared that no other chimney-pot in the United Kingdom, broken or unbroken, could be so beautiful as the one at No. 48.[14]

That was in Great Coram Street—not very far from Doughty Street, and it is quite extraordinary that Dickens should have anticipated that number. In fact, he had done so before in an even earlier story, 'Horatio Sparkins', also published in *The Monthly Magazine*, in February 1834, and later in *Sketches by Boz*. One wonders whether 48 was a magic number for Dickens: 'Mr Sparkins bowed, and promised to join the party in box 48 in the course of the evening.'[15]

Dickens was attracted to Doughty Street because it was a private road with a gateway at each end, and consequently reasonably quiet as far as traffic was concerned. On duty at each gate was a porter or beadle in mulberry-coloured uniform and gold-laced hat, with the Doughty Arms on his buttons. Dickens may have seen this prior to moving into Doughty Street—hence the character Job Trotter in *Pickwick Papers*, in a similar-coloured suit. (Job Trotter made his first appearance in Part Six, Chapter 16, about August 1836.)

Dickens was obviously referring to his Doughty Street experiences in his paper 'Some Recollections of Mortality' which appeared in *All The Year Round*, on 16 May 1863, and later in the collection known as *The Uncommercial Traveller*:

The thing happened say five-and-twenty years ago [1838]. I was a modest young commercial then, and timid and inexperienced. Many suns and winds have browned me in the line, but those were my pale days. Having newly taken the lease of a house in a certain distinguished metropolitan parish—a house which then appeared to me to be a frightfully first-class Family Mansion, involving awful responsibilities—I become the prey of a Beadle. I think the Beadle must have seen me going in or coming out, and must have observed that I tottered under the weight of my grandeur. Or he may have been in hiding under the straw when I bought my first horse (in the desirable stable-yard attached to the first-class Family Mansion) and when the vendor remarked to me, in an original manner, on bringing him for approval, taking his cloth off and smacking him, 'There, Sir! *There's* a Orse!' And I said gallantly, 'How much do you want for him?' and when the vendor said, 'No more than sixty guineas, from you,' and when I said smartly, 'Why no more than sixty from me?' And when he said crushingly, 'Because upon my soul and body he'd be considered cheap at seventy, by one who understood the subject—but you don't!'—I say, the Beadle may have been in hiding under straw, when this disgrace befell me, or he may have noted that I was too raw and young an Atlas to carry the first-class Family Mansion in a knowing manner. Be this as it may, the Beadle did what Melancholy did to the Youth in Gray's Elegy—he marked me for his own.

> [*Here rests his head upon the lap of earth*
> *A youth to fortune and to fame unknown.*
> *Fair Science frown'd not on his humble birth,*
> *And Melancholy mark'd him for his own.*]

And the way in which the Beadle did it, was this: he summoned me as a Juryman on his Coroner's Inquests.

In my first feverish alarm I repaired 'for safety and succour'—like those sagacious Northern shepherds, who, having had no previous reason whatever to believe in young Norval, very prudently did not originate the hazardous idea of believing in him—to a deep householder. This profound man informed me that the Beadle counted on my buying him off; on my bribing him not to summon me; and that if I would attend an Inquest with a cheerful countenance, and profess alacrity in that branch of my country's service, the Beadle would be disheartened and would give up the game.

I roused my energies and the next time the wily Beadle summoned me, I went. The Beadle was the blankest Beadle I have ever looked on when I answered to my name; and his discomfiture gave me courage to go through with it.[16]

There follows a sad account of an enquiry into the death of a very little mite of a child, to decide whether the mother had committed the minor offence of concealing the birth, or whether she had committed the major offence of killing the child. At the inquest, Dickens, encouraged by the coroner, asked various questions, as a result of which the minor offence was agreed against the mother. In conclusion, Dickens says:

> I regard this as a very notable uncommercial experience because this good came of a Beadle. And to the best of my knowledge, information and belief, it is the only good that ever did come of a Beadle, since the first Beadle put on his cocked hat.[17]

About this time Dickens pilloried beadles in no uncertain manner by creating that famous representative of all beadles, Mr Bumble, who has given us a word in our English language—Bumbledom—and whose famous remark '... the law is a ass—a idiot'[18] is as well known and possibly as often quoted as little Oliver's famous plea—'Please, sir, I want some more'.[19]

The mews where Dickens got his horses has been partly rebuilt and converted to small industry, but in parts the original cobblestones can still be trodden and the original kennel runs along the centre. These are now called Brownlow Mews after the genial old character in *Oliver Twist*.

On one occasion Dickens wrote to his friend Harrison Ainsworth, an historical novelist, that they would mount their horses on the following Sunday, no doubt to the disappointment of the neighbours opposite, at the mews where the animals were kept and that Serjeant Talfourd, their barrister friend, would be put on his horse at his own residence.[20] Possibly Dickens's suggestion that they should not mount their horses in view of the neighbours was made because of the criticism of a Mrs Touchet, Ainsworth's housekeeper, who was an experienced horsewoman in the hunting field. It also reminds one of Mr Winkle mounting his horse on the wrong side with 'as much difficulty as he would have experienced in getting up the side of a first-rate man-of-war'.[21]

Whilst Dickens was at Doughty Street he appeared as a witness in Bow Street Court in a case against Richard Davis, proprietor of Omnibus No. 3861. Davis was summoned to appear before Mr Twyford by Mr Thorne, Secretary of the Society for the Prevention of Cruelty to Animals. Davis was accused of cruelly beating and ill-treating a horse when it was unfit for work. Mr Wright, a solicitor from the Temple, gave evidence against the omnibus proprietor and Dickens supported him, pointing out that a very large portion of the horse's shoulder was completely raw. The defendant was fined 20s. and costs.[22]

It is certain that there were at least four members of domestic staff at Doughty Street—a cook, a housemaid, a nurse and a manservant. The nurse's wages seemed to vary and to be somewhat erratically paid, at least according to those details recorded, though of course her wages may have been included in the sundry items against 'House' or 'Mrs Dickens' without being entered separately. The nurse's monthly wages varied from £3 to £4 5s. The cook's wages again varied in amount and frequency of payment, and start at £3 13s. 6d. per month, in 1838, rising sometimes to £4 17s. or falling to lower figures such as (14 May) £2 7s. and (28 August 1839) £3 10s. Perhaps she was paid extra when Dickens entertained. The housemaid's wages were more consistent, starting at $2\frac{1}{2}$ guineas in 1838 and rising to 3 guineas in January 1839, which rate seems to have been maintained.[23]

Occasional payments marked 'Stable' indicate Dickens's riding activities, but no reference to the manservant, Henry, or to William Topping, the groom, appears in the bank book. Henry was dismissed in February 1839, and Topping replaced him on 2 March. No doubt numerous little 'tweenies' were employed from the nearby orphanage, as scullery maids at 2*s.* or 2*s.* 6*d.* a week, who were thankful enough to get a good home. Just after leaving Doughty Street, Dickens immortalized these little unfortunates in the delightful character of the Marchioness in *The Old Curiosity Shop*, but it is hardly likely that they were treated in the Dickens household as she was.

> Miss Brass took a key from her pocket, and opening the safe, brought from it a dreary waste of cold potatoes, looking as eatable as Stonehenge. This she placed before the small servant, ordering her to sit down before it, and then, taking up a great carving-knife, made a mighty show of sharpening it upon the carving-fork.
>
> 'Do you see this?' said Miss Brass, slicing off about two square inches of cold mutton, after all this preparation, and holding it out on the point of the fork. The small servant looked hard enough at it with her hungry eyes to see every shred of it, small as it was, and answered, 'Yes.'
>
> 'Then don't you ever go and say,' retorted Miss Sally, 'that you hadn't meat here. There, eat it up.'[24]

Who could better that description of cold potatoes 'as eatable as Stonehenge'? These little slaveys were introduced many times—Mrs Tibbs's servant, in 'The Boarding House' (*Sketches by Boz*), for example, or Mrs Raddle's servant— 'a dirty slipshod girl in black cotton stockings, who might have passed for the neglected daughter of a superannuated dustman in very reduced circumstances'.[25] They all seemed to suffer from a perpetual sniff!

On the morning of the birth of Charley, Dickens's eldest son, when Kate's labour began, Dickens and Mary were sent out of the way by the two mothers to find a small table for Kate to have at her bedside. In the first shop they came to, they saw what appeared to be a suitable table, but Dickens could not pluck up courage to go in and ask the price. After wandering up and down Holborn and sundry side streets for some hours, they eventually bought the table they had seen at first.[26]

The baby was named Culliford after Dickens's maternal great-uncle, and the name 'Boz' came to be added because John Dickens was said to have shouted it out in church after the baby's godfather had given the first name.[27]

Dickens used his furniture-seeking experiences in humorous vein in later writings, as, for example, in the fictional shopping expeditions of David and Dora, assisted by Dora's aunts;[28] or Traddles shopping with Clara Peggotty and endeavouring to buy back his own property—the little round table with the marble top, and Sophy's flower-pot and stand, which had been seized by the bailiff for Mr Micawber's debts;[29] or when Miss Charity Pecksniff went shopping with Augustus Moddle, for the eight rosewood chairs and the loo table.[30]

In her description of the Dickens household at Furnival's Inn, Mary described the rooms as being most tastefully and elegantly furnished, the drawing-room with rosewood, the dining-room with mahogany furniture. This gives a broad idea of the furnishing at Doughty Street, for undoubtedly the same pieces were used in their new home. After their next move, to 1 Devonshire Terrace, much of the cheaper bedroom furniture may have been passed on to the servants and better pieces purchased.

There is, for instance, in the Dickens House Museum, a handsome Spanish mahogany sideboard, which was purchased by Dickens whilst he was at Doughty Street, with the larger house (in which richer furniture could be displayed to better advantage) in mind. This sideboard was in the family until Dickens died, and can be seen in the photograph taken of the dining-room at Gad's Hill Place, after his death. Disposed of in the Gad's Hill sale, it eventually reached America; its last owner very generously presented it to the Dickens House Museum, so it is now back in its original home.

At the back of this sideboard is a large mirror, typical of the mirrors with which Dickens liked to surround himself. This was not, as sometimes suggested, because of his vanity, but because he liked to have light and brightness around him. This is understandable, for in his day evenings had to be spent in the dim light of a candle or oil lamp, which to us would seem semi-darkness. When Dickens furnished the Swiss Chalet in the grounds of Gad's Hill Place, Rochester, as a summer study, he had mirrors on all the walls to reflect the bright sky and trees outside the windows.

There is also a smaller sideboard, said to have belonged to Dickens when at Doughty Street, and now in the Dickens House at Broadstairs. It was possibly the one replaced by the larger sideboard, now at Doughty Street. It has the lion's-head motif on the drawer handles, a device to which Dickens seemed to be rather partial.

One other piece of furniture in the (London) Dickens House Museum, an armchair, was at Doughty Street when he was. George Cruikshank drew a portrait in 1837 of Dickens sitting in it.[31] Dickens's first task on moving into the Doughty Street house would have been to arrange and re-arrange all the furniture to his liking. This was something he always did when going into a new place, lodging, hotel, or whatever. His bed always had to be in a certain direction. That done to his satisfaction, he could settle down, as far as this restless, dynamic being ever settled down, to enjoy his own first real home.

There are sundry miscellaneous entries in his bank book, which is on display in the museum at Doughty Street, which point to his way of life whilst in that house. He belonged, for instance, to several clubs, and entry fees and subscriptions to the Garrick Club, the Parthenon Club and the Athenaeum are recorded. There are also donations to various charities, in addition to the Theatrical and Artists' Benevolent Funds (see Chapter 12), The (nearby) Foundling Hospital, The Literary Friendly Society, The Literary Fund, The Newspaper Press Benevolent Association and the Charitable Commission; all these recurring regularly over the period he was at Doughty Street.[32]

Substantial premium payments to the Britannia Life Assurance Co. point to the fact that in spite of his rejection by another company, because he was working too hard, he did have his life insured.[33]

In his bank book a payment is recorded against the name of Huffam, his godfather, and it seems likely that Dickens might have helped him financially, when he was able to do so.[34] Many members of his family certainly looked to him for help during his life, and he responded generously. It is certainly not a fact—as some people seem inclined to think —that he deserted his family or shirked his obligations.

The large Family Bible lent by the Dickens family to the Dickens House Museum, and on display there, is open at the page on which Dickens recorded the births and deaths of his family of ten children. The births relating to Doughty

Street are those of his daughters: 'Mary Dickens, 6 March 1838; Kate Macready Dickens, 29 October 1839.' Both survived him, and their deaths were recorded by later members of the family.[35] A family tree, on the wall above the case containing the Bible and Dickens's Special Marriage Licence (his bride was under age), traces the Dickens family from John and Elizabeth down to the present generation.[36] There are more than eighty descendants, but only twelve still bear the name of Dickens.

CHAPTER 2

'The dearest friend I ever had'

THE younger lady was in the lovely bloom and springtime of woman-hood; at that age, when, if ever angels be for God's good purposes, enthroned in mortal forms, they may be, without impiety, supposed to abide in such as hers. *Oh! where are the hearts which following some halting description of youth and beauty, do not recal* [sic] *a loved original that Time has sadly changed, or Death resolved to dust.* She was not past seventeen. Cast in so slight and exquisite a mould; so mild and gentle; so pure and beautiful; that earth seemed not her element, nor its rough creatures her fit companions. The very intelligence that shone in her deep blue eye, and was stamped upon her noble head, seemed scarcely of her age or of the world; and yet the changing expression of sweetness and good humour; the thousand lights that played about the face, and left no shadow there; above all, the smile; the cheerful, happy smile; were made for Home; for fireside peace and Happiness.[1]

Obviously, the above passage is by the same writer as the following epitaph, with the same person in mind:

Young, Beautiful, and Good,
God in His Mercy
Numbered Her With His Angels
At the early age of
Seventeen.

The description from *Oliver Twist* is of Rose Maylie (the passage in italics appeared in the manuscript, but was omitted from the text of the book). There is no doubt that when Dickens wrote this description in April 1838, in Chapter 29 of *Oliver Twist*, he was thinking once more of Mary Hogarth, his young sister-in-law.

Dickens was supremely happy when he moved into Doughty Street, and had every reason to be so. *Pickwick Papers* was almost two-thirds written, he was editor of a magazine—*Bentley's Miscellany*, the second or third instalment of *Oliver Twist* was behind him, an operetta completed and being produced in a London theatre, and two other short plays were in production: he began to feel that life was good to him.

Now, at Doughty Street, he knew that it was not just a question of one book, but that he could go on writing more stories and creating those remarkable characters. He was beginning to become famous and there was every prospect that he would be able to earn his living in the literary world.

At the end of March 1837, he celebrated the first anniversary of the publication of *Pickwick Papers*. The book had surpassed the publishers' most optimistic dreams and Chapman and Hall, wishing to share their good fortune with this young author, sent him an honorarium of £500 over and above the agreed advance, and gave a dinner to celebrate the anniversary, which took place on 8 April.

After the wedding of Dickens and Catherine Hogarth (Kate), her sister Mary stayed with them at Furnival's Inn, and came to live with them permanently when they moved to 48 Doughty Street. This arrangement was quite usual in those days; often, after weddings, the bridesmaid would even go away on the honeymoon with the bride and bridegroom. It will be remembered that after Mr Lillyvick married Miss Henrietta Petowker of Drury Lane, the Infant Phenomenon, who was their bridesmaid, went away with them on their honeymoon. Also John Browdie and his wife in the same book, *Nicholas Nickleby*, were accompanied on their honeymoon to London by Fanny Squeers, their bridesmaid. Mary Hogarth had often accompanied Catherine and Charles as chaperon, and after their marriage Dickens naturally accepted her being there in their home.

Whilst her sister Kate tended to be dull and lethargic, especially during her pregnancy, Mary was bright and vivacious. Dickens could not find praise enough to bestow upon her. As he wrote in a letter to Thomas Beard, 'I solemnly believe that so perfect a creature never breathed'.[2]

With this intelligent young girl as his constant companion providing an interested and appreciative audience to his efforts, giving him the encouragement he needed, his happiness was complete. Then, suddenly, without the slightest warning, he suffered perhaps the greatest blow of his life. One Saturday night, at the beginning of May 1837, Dickens, accompanied by his wife and Mary, went to St James's Theatre to a performance of his operetta, *The Village Coquettes*. Returning from the theatre, warmed and thrilled at seeing the presentation of Dickens's own creation on the stage, they came home to Doughty Street. Cheerful laughter, a few happy goodnights and Mary ran lightly upstairs to her second-floor bedroom, leaving the others to put out the lights and follow to their front bedroom, which was next to hers. Hardly had she gained her room when suddenly Dickens heard a strange, strangled cry. He rushed upstairs, followed by Kate, into Mary's room where they found her very ill, suffering from some unaccountable attack. Fred was sent out to fetch the doctor, who, when he came, could apparently give no help. (It is not clear which doctor attended, although Dickens's family doctor, referred to by him as his usual medical attendant, was Francis Peregrine Pickthorn.[3])

Dickens wrote in a letter to an unknown correspondent some time after the event that although every effort was made to save Mary, and no danger apprehended until nearly the very last, she sank under the attack, dying in such a calm and gentle sleep that although he had held her in his arms for some time before, when she was certainly living, he continued to support her lifeless form long after her soul had fled to Heaven.[4] She died at about three o'clock on the Sunday afternoon, 7 May 1837.

Letter after letter, on deep-black bordered notepaper, he wrote to various people—Edward Chapman, George Thomson (Mary's maternal grandfather), Harrison Ainsworth, Richard Bentley, Thomas Beard, Thomas Mitton and John Forster, pouring out his heart in his great sorrow. To Richard Johns, writer and contributor to *Bentley's Miscellany*, he wrote:

> From the day of our marriage the dear girl had been the grace and life of our home, our constant companion, and the sharer of all our little pleasures. The love and affection which subsisted between her and her sister, no one can imagine the extent of. We might have known that we were too happy together to be long without a change. The change has come, and it has fallen heavily upon us. I have lost the dearest friend I ever had. Words cannot describe the pride I felt in her, and the devoted

attachment I bore her. She well deserved it, for with abilities far beyond her years, with every attraction of youth and beauty, and conscious as she must have been of everybody's admiration, she had not a single fault, and was in life almost as far above the foibles and vanity of her sex and age as she is now in Heaven.[5]

In announcing her sudden death to Mary's grandfather, Dickens said that the doctors were of the opinion that her heart had been diseased for a long time.[6] It seems strange that she does not appear to have had any warning symptoms prior to her fatal attack, nor does she seem to have been undergoing any medical treatment.

Mrs Hogarth had been hastily summoned to Doughty Street and was there when her daughter died. The shock caused her to lose consciousness and she remained insensible for a week afterwards—another anxiety for the young couple. Dickens took a ring from Mary's finger and wore it for the rest of his life, a ring which is still in the Dickens family's possession. He kept her clothes to look at, which recalls the old grandfather after the death of Little Nell, taking out her dress and shoes:

'Her little homely dress,—her favourite! She will miss it when she wakes. They have hid it here in sport, but she shall have it—she shall have it ...'[7]

The funeral, for which Dickens paid, was on 13 May, at Kensal Green Cemetery. Referring to the funeral Dickens wrote:

I feel that as tomorrow draws nigh, the bitterest part of this calamity is at hand. I hope that for that one day at all events I may be able to bear my part in it with fortitude, and to encourage and console those about me—it will be no harder trial to anyone than myself.[8]

It seems never to have occurred to him that others may have felt the loss as much as he did—her mother in the loss of a daughter, or his wife in the loss of her sister. He was obliged to borrow money, or rather obtain an advance from Edward Chapman, to meet the expense of the funeral. One wonders what had happened to the £500 he had received from Chapman and Hall only a month before Mary's death.

It appears to have been an expensive funeral, no doubt with all the trappings and ostentation expected by the neighbours. No one would dare do otherwise—the black velvet pall, the nodding black ostrich plumes on the hearse and the horses, the crêpe and black-bordered handkerchiefs. Dickens's experience of this and later funerals he attended must have contributed to the outspoken comments on such hollow mockery which appear in his novels. For instance, when he wrote of Pip's sister's funeral in *Great Expectations*, he had grown important enough to speak his mind:

> The air of the parlour being faint with the smell of sweet cake, I looked about for the table of refreshments; it was scarcely visible until one had got accustomed to the gloom, but there was cut-up plum cake upon it, and there were cut-up oranges, and sandwiches and biscuits, and two decanters . . . one full of port and one of sherry.

There was Mr Trabb, the local tailor and undertaker, holding a kind of black bazaar, with the aid of a quantity of black pins and putting somebody's hat into black long-clothes, like an African baby.

> 'Which I meantersay, Pip,' Joe whispered to me, as we were being what Mr Trabb called 'formed' in the parlour, two and two—and it was dreadfully like a preparation for some grim kind of dance; 'Which I meantersay, sir, as I would in preference have carried her to the church myself, along with three or four friendly ones wot come to it with willing harts and arms, but it were considered wot the neighbours would look down on such and would be of opinion as it were wanting in respect.' 'Pocket handkerchiefs out all,' cried Mr Trabb . . . So we all put our pocket handkerchiefs to our faces, as if our noses were bleeding, and filed out two and two . . . it being a point of undertaking ceremony that the six bearers must be stifled and blinded under a horrible black housing with twelve human legs, shuffling and blundering along.

Then, suddenly, the grim comedy dies and genuine feeling takes its place:

> And now the range of marshes lay before us, with the sails of the ships on the river growing out of it; and we went into the churchyard . . . and there my sister was laid quietly in the earth, while the larks sung high above it, and the light wind strewed it with the beautiful shadows of clouds and trees.[9]

But until such times as the trappings and customs of such events could be relaxed, it was necessary to follow the conventions of the times, as after the death of Steerforth in *David Copperfield* ('I went through the dreary house, and darkened the windows . . .'). All this must have been experienced by Dickens at Doughty Street, while thoughts built up in his mind that were later to be used so brilliantly in his stories.

Finding that he was unable to settle down to his usual monthly routine, he decided to go away for a fortnight's rest. There was therefore no number of *Pickwick Papers* at the end of May, nor the instalment of *Oliver Twist* in the June issue of *Bentley's Miscellany*. Instead of the usual instalment of *Oliver Twist*, the following notice appeared:

> Since the appearance of the last number of this work the editor has to mourn the sudden death of a very dear young relative to whom he was most affectionately attached and whose society has been for a long time the chief solace of his labours.

In spite of this notice all sorts of rumours were passed round. On resuming his work on 30 June, therefore, he issued the following address:

> By one set of intimate acquaintances, especially well-informed, he has been killed outright; by another driven mad; by a third, imprisoned for debt; by a fourth, sent per steamer to the United States; by a fifth, rendered incapable of mental exertion for evermore; by all, in short, represented as doing anything but seeking in a few weeks' retirement the restoration of that cheerfulness and peace of which a sad bereavement had temporarily deprived him.[10]

Kate, who as so often was pregnant, after the shock of her sister's sudden death and the worry of her mother's condition, suffered a miscarriage and her husband decided to take her away. This he did, and they stayed at Collins's Farm (sometimes known as Wylde's Farm) at North End, Hampstead. The building is still preserved by the side of the Heath. Later, in the story of *Oliver Twist*, Dickens was to use North End Village as the place where Bill Sikes slept under the hedge after escaping from London, following the brutal murder of Nancy.

For many months after Mary's death Dickens dreamed about her—

> sometimes as a spirit, sometimes as a living creature, never with any of the bitterness of my real sorrow, but always with a kind of quiet happiness, which became so pleasant to me that I never lay down at night without a hope of the vision coming back in one shape or other. And so

it did. I went down into Yorkshire, and finding it still present to me in a strange scene and a strange bed, I could not help mentioning the circumstances in a note I wrote home to Kate. From that moment I have never dreamed of her once, though she is so much in my thoughts at all times (especially when I am successful and have prospered in anything), that the recollection of her is an essential part of my being, and is as inseparable from my being as the beating of my heart is.[11]

At all great moments in his life he remembered her. One instance was when he was standing beside Niagara Falls during his first visit to America, in 1842.

There was a bright rainbow at my feet; and from that I looked up to—great Heaven! to *what* a fall of bright green water! The broad, deep, mighty stream seems to die in the act of falling; and, from its unfathomable grave, arises that tremendous ghost of spray and mist which is never laid, and has been haunting this place with the same dread solemnity—perhaps from the creation of the world ... what would I give if the dear girl whose ashes lie in Kensal-green, had lived to come so far along with us—but she has been here many times, I doubt not, since her sweet face faded from my earthly sight.[12]

When he was in Genoa, however, in 1844, he dreamed of her again, or thought he did:

I was visited by a spirit, I could not make out the face ... It wore a blue drapery, as the Madonna might in a picture by Raphael; and bore no resemblance to anyone I have known except in stature. I think (but I am not sure) that I recognized the voice. Anyway, I knew it was poor Mary's spirit. I was not at all afraid, but in great delight, so that I wept very much, and stretching out my arms to it called it 'Dear.'[13]

Unable to get her out of his thoughts, about a month after she died he went again to the cemetery and wrote to an unknown person:

Her body lies in the beautiful cemetery in the Harrow Road. I saw her grave but a few days ago, and the grass around it was as green and the flowers as bright, as if nothing of the earth in which they grew could ever wither or fade. Beneath my feet there lay a silent but solemn witness that all health and beauty are but things of the hour. Mrs Hogarth has suffered and still suffers deeply from this dreadful calamity. For her who is dead I can feel no sorrow, for I know that before a single care of life had wounded her pure heart, she has passed quietly away to an immortality of happiness and joy. Those who are left behind to recollect what she was here; to miss her sweet face and her winning smile, and all the countless endearments that a guileless heart and affectionate nature gave birth to, are indeed objects for sympathy and compassion. Among these mourners as none loved her better living, so, believe me, none laments her more constantly and deeply in death, than, My Dear Sir Yours most affectionately and faithfully Charles Dickens.[14]

The epitaph on Mary's gravestone, written by Dickens, became very badly worn by the rain dripping on it from the trees above. Some years ago it was restored by a member of the family and later by the Dickens Fellowship. Now, thanks to the generosity of an American member of the Fellowship (the late Arnold Ziegler), a sum of money has been provided to maintain the inscription for all time.

Dickens had always hoped that he could be buried in Mary's grave, but when her brother George died suddenly in 1841, he wrote to Mrs Hogarth:

I will cheerfully arrange to place the ground at your entire disposal. Do not consider me in any way. Consult only your own heart. Mine seems to tell me that as they both died so young and so suddenly, they ought both to be buried together.[15]

Unable to obtain any ground on either side of the grave and reluctant to have Mary's body moved, in deference to the family, he realized that he would have to give up any idea of being buried in the same grave, or near to Mary. He sadly gazed upon her coffin for the last time when the grave was opened for George's burial.

This morbid streak in Dickens has been something of a puzzle to biographers, but he certainly possessed it and this was evidenced in his writings when bubbling humour sometimes alternated with harrowing death scenes, often involving the very young. His obsession with his young sister-in-law, after only knowing her for two or three years, and his deep sorrow at her loss, which apparently even time could not heal, has proved a difficult problem to explain. That he married the wrong sister (as is sometimes suggested) is scarcely a feasible explanation, for Mary was hardly more than a schoolgirl when Dickens first came into the Hogarth family. That with her, it was a case of hero-worship is quite understandable. This brilliant young genius who burst upon the family could hardly fail to rouse such feelings in the heart and mind of a young girl, who till then perhaps

2

had led a somewhat sheltered life. He undoubtedly married in haste—on the rebound, as it were, and smarting under his treatment at the hands of the flirtatious Maria Beadnell.

It seems to be accepted without question that on neither side did physical attraction enter into the association. On hers, it was purely hero-worship, and on his, the acceptance of her as an ideal, a symbol perhaps of female perfection—not only what she was, but what he made her in his imagination. Professor Wagenknecht sums up the situation neatly when he says : 'Mary was hardly a woman to him at all: she was an ideal, and she remained in that light to the end of his days.'

How far, one wonders, did this idealism of his wife's sister affect his marital relationship with Kate in later years? Only in one letter, to Harrison Ainsworth, did he put his wife first, and a wife to whom he had been married for just over a year, referring to Mary as the dear girl whom he loved, after his wife, more deeply and fervently than anyone on earth.[16] On all other occasions he holds Mary up as one he loved above everyone else. Surely that must have had some effect upon his wife's feelings.

Little Nell is supposed to be the character who above all others was based on Mary Hogarth, because Dickens himself particularly referred to her in this light. As he approached the end of *The Old Curiosity Shop*, he wrote to Forster:

> ... this part of the story is not to be galloped over, I can tell you. I think it will come famously—but I am the wretchedest of the wretched. It casts the most horrible shadow upon me, and it is as much as I can do to keep moving at all. I tremble to approach the place a great deal more than Kit; a great deal more than Mr Garland; a great deal more than the Single Gentleman. I shan't recover from it for a long time. Nobody will miss her like I shall. It is such a very painful thing to me, that I really cannot express my sorrow. Old wounds bleed afresh when I only think of the way of doing it: what the actual thing will be, God knows. I can't preach to myself the schoolmaster's consolation, though I try. Dear Mary died yesterday, when I think of this sad story.[17]

That was nearly four years after Mary's death.

In many other characters there were traces of Mary Hogarth: 'She was very young, apparently no more than seventeen ... her figure was slight ... but all the charm of youth and maidenhood set it off.' (Mary Graham in *Martin Chuzzlewit*); 'So she *is* an angel, Captain. If there is an angel anywhere, it's Miss Dombey.' (Florence Dombey in *Dombey and Son*); 'Her beautiful serene eyes met mine ... her angel-face was turned upon me.' (Agnes Wickfield in *David Copperfield*); 'a young lady of not more than seventeen ... short, slight, pretty figure.' (Lucy Manette in *A Tale of Two Cities*)—many perhaps rather colourless creations, but moulded on that ideal in Dickens's mind, and many of them Mary's age—seventeen.

There is more resemblance in Rose Maylie, in *Oliver Twist*, because she was introduced only a year after Mary's death (and she, too, was seventeen). Was Dickens perhaps actually describing Mary's symptoms in Rose's illness?

> ... the hue of her countenance had changed to a marble whiteness. Its expression had lost nothing of its beauty; but it was changed; and there was an anxious, haggard look about the gentle face, which it had never worn before. Another minute, and it was suffused with a crimson flush: and a heavy wildness came over the soft blue eyes again; again this disappeared, like the shadow thrown by a passing cloud: and she was once more deadly pale.[18]
>
> 'Heaven,' says Oliver, 'will never let her die so young.'

Rose Maylie recovers in the story, because although Dickens was obviously torturing himself by creating her and introducing her illness, he could not bring himself at that time, to kill this character moulded so closely on Mary Hogarth. The sudden death of this young girl in Doughty Street was undoubtedly one of the greatest influences on his work and was to a great extent responsible for the heavy sentiment which pervaded his writings. In many of his books after *Pickwick Papers*, the influence of Dickens's memory of Mary Hogarth can be seen in many of his young female characters. As J. W. T. Ley said in his article in the 1937 *Dickensian*, on the centenary of Mary's death: 'She is part of the world's literature.'

CHAPTER 3

Uneasy partnerships

To follow the difficulties and disputes Dickens had with his early publishers, it is necessary to glance at his career prior to the Doughty Street days. He had contributed sundry sketches and stories to *The Monthly Magazine* and other publications, without payment, and after being appointed Parliamentary Reporter for the *Morning Chronicle*, at 5 guineas a week, had agreed to contribute sketches to the *Evening Chronicle*, for which he was to receive a further 2 guineas.

Harrison Ainsworth had introduced Dickens to his own publisher, John Macrone, who arranged to publish a collection of these sketches in volume form, illustrated by George Cruikshank, and which were to be known as *Sketches by Boz*. Dickens's young brother Augustus had been nicknamed Moses from *The Vicar of Wakefield*. Moses pronounced by the seven-year-old Augustus became 'Boses', which became shortened to 'Bose', hence the pseudonym adopted by Dickens—Boz. For this publication by Macrone, Dickens was to be paid £150.

These *Sketches*, the importance of which perhaps Dickens himself underrated when referring to them later, may have done more to establish him as a writer than was appreciated at the time. They contain rough outlines of characters such as Sam Weller, Bumble and Mrs Gamp, which were later so brilliantly 'filled in' and perfected. The Tales which form part of the book do, with their superficial music-hall plots, show signs of the immature young reporter's first literary efforts, but in the descriptive passages the *Sketches* show inklings of the novelist's latent literary power, and flashes of genius to come. In gathering them together in the two volumes, Macrone did valuable work in establishing Dickens's name, although it was at first only under a pseudonym. It is significant that John Forster in his biography of Dickens says 'The *Sketches* were much more talked about than the first two or three numbers of *Pickwick* ... He decidedly underrated it ...' Even at this early stage in his career Dickens was perhaps setting his sights on the eventual production of a three-volume novel on a par with those already to the credit of Harrison Ainsworth and Edward Bulwer (later Lord Lytton). He seemed almost to be taking retrogade steps at first in undertaking the serialization of *Pickwick Papers* in monthly parts; but that was to change as he went on.

Chapman and Hall had agreed to pay Dickens in respect of *Pickwick Papers* 9 guineas per sheet of 16 pages demy octavo, containing about 500 words on a page. They would require a sheet and a half every month, so that the author would receive about 14 guineas.[1]

Dickens had evidently been trying to make some arrangements with *The Sunday Times*, but was unsuccessful and had resigned himself to spending another period as reporter in the gallery of the House of Commons.[2] He was very anxious to be relieved of all the tough journeying he had been doing at all hours; but without the certainty of a steady income to replace his 7 guineas a week from the newspaper, he could not make a change.

At this point he had tied himself up with two publishers, but all the arrangements made were for the future and none of them would be of any immediate benefit to his income, which was what he really sought. Furthermore, all the arrangements made were based on his value as an almost unknown writer, and made no allowance for his value increasing as he became more popular. In view of his meteoric rise with the publication of *Pickwick Papers*, his signing of these contracts was, to say the least of it, very unwise. But of course he was inexperienced, and no doubt dazzled by the willingness of publishers to deal with him and accept his work in the future.

First was the agreement to write *Pickwick Papers* for Chapman and Hall, which was to bring him in a steady income. Dickens also entered into an arrangement with Chapman and Hall that he should write a second novel, on the completion of *Pickwick Papers*, for each monthly

number of which he was to be paid £150. This book became
Nicholas Nickleby, and in this case his increased value had
certainly been taken into consideration by Chapman and
Hall. Generally speaking, after his earlier books, and once
he had broken the shackles of the low remuneration resulting
from contracts into which he had entered somewhat thought-
lessly, he was paid at a rate much higher than that received
by many, or possibly all of his contemporaries in the literary
world. Dickens had promised to write a three-volume novel
for Macrone, to be entitled *Gabriel Varden, Locksmith of
London*, for which he was to be paid £200 plus part of the
profits of all numbers sold over one thousand, delivery of
the manuscript to be on or before 30 November 1836.[3]

He had also agreed to write a three-volume novel for
Richard Bentley for £500, payable in two instalments of
£200 each and a final one of £100. This was payable on
sales reaching 1450 copies. Copyright was to be assigned to
Bentley and no other literary production was to be undertaken.[4] Dickens was also to offer a second novel to Bentley,
on the same terms.

He had therefore got himself into a pretty considerable
mess with little likelihood of being able to deliver the goods.
The situation, looked back on from the distance of 140
years, was almost farcical, but to a young inexperienced
author, still learning the art of literature, it must have
appeared anything but funny; yet he continued accepting
commissions which, had he stopped to think, he should
have known he could not possibly fulfil.

Just when Dickens was despairing of being able to give
up the rigours of journalism, Bentley decided to publish a
new magazine, first called *The Wit's Miscellany* and later
Bentley's Miscellany, which led to Theodore Hook's remark
that the title 'Miss-sell-any' was an ill-chosen one. Theodore
Hook was a writer and lampoonist who later had business
connections with Dickens, but his predictions about
Bentley's Miscellany were proved wrong.

Bentley invited Dickens to become its editor on the
following terms: the editor was to be paid £20 per month,
to correspond with literary men with a view to attracting
suitable articles, to read articles submitted, give judgment,
and to revise and correct those accepted. He was also to

write original articles himself of 16 pages, at £21 per sheet. Copyright of any such articles or stories to be assigned to Bentley. No other agreement was to be made apart from that with Chapman and Hall to write another novel for them on the completion of *Pickwick*.[5] Payment for the editorship and authorship of *Bentley's Miscellany* was 75 per cent higher than the payment for *Pickwick*, which shows that in this case cognizance was taken of Dickens's increased popularity and value as an author.

A further agreement with Bentley provided for an additional payment of £10 for each monthly number of the *Miscellany* when sales exceeded 6000, and a further £5 for every succeeding 500 beyond the 6000.[6] With over £300 per annum coming in from *Pickwick Papers*, the arrangements with Bentley increased Dickens's income to about £800 per annum and he could at last afford to abandon his 7 guineas weekly for his newspaper work. Indeed, he could hardly carry out all these tasks—write *Pickwick*, edit *Bentley's Miscellany* and write a story for it, and fulfil his journalistic duties. Here came his break with journalism, although in one sense he undoubtedly remained a journalist all his life, with his vivid powers of description—his ability not only to describe what he was seeing or imagining, but to convey a picture to the minds of his readers, with his brilliant choice of words. The reader can see things happening, hear the characters talking and almost smell those meals cooking!

In a letter to John Easthope, one of the proprietors of *The Morning Chronicle*, Dickens tendered quite a reasonably expressed notice to resign, though perhaps he did not give the newspaper much time to adjust its staff. He was quite within his rights to give such short notice, however, as the newspaper would have been had they dismissed him.

In inclosing to you, the accompanying letter to the Proprietors of *The Morning Chronicle*, I am anxious to express to you personally, my warmest and most sincere thanks for all the courtesies and kindnesses I have received at your hands. Although I exchange for a less burdensome and more profitable employment, I can assure you that I feel great regret in leaving an Establishment where I have uniformly discharged my duties with so much pleasure to myself, and I hope I may add, with so much satisfaction to my Employers.

Dickens did rather jump the gun here, leaving his employers with little to say. He continued:

> Notwithstanding that my time will not be very much occupied immediately, I have deemed it right to beg you to accept my notice from to-day. I only concluded my other arrangements this morning, or I should have given it before. The additional salary, if you please, will now cease. Between this time, and the period at which my notice will expire, I shall take care to make the number of sketches bear the proper proportion to the amount I have received. I should be happy to speak to you further, on this subject, if you will have the goodness to write me word when I may hope to see you at the Office.[7]

The additional salary mentioned was the 2 guineas to be paid for the sketches contributed to the *Evening Chronicle*. Dickens had received 6 guineas in respect of sketches he had not written, hence his offer to provide these sketches and make them 'bear the proper proportion to the amount [he had] received'.

Easthope, obviously annoyed at the loss of the services of a very valuable reporter—as Dickens certainly had become at that time—replied in a very unfriendly tone, criticizing Dickens for having left the office without seeing him and for having accepted payment for three sketches which had not been provided—in spite of Dickens's offer to write them.

In a long reply to Easthope, Dickens explained that he did not intend to be discourteous, but that on that day he had left Mrs Dickens in a shop and did not wish to leave her longer in a strange place than he could help—hence his abrupt departure. As he proceeded with this letter he became more and more annoyed, especially when he thought of the unwritten sketches and all he had done for the paper, presumably without thanks from his employers. In regard to the sketches he said:

> I have only to add that I shall return the six guineas with the utmost pleasure, and that I wish I could return at the same time every additional sixpence beyond my regular Salary as a reporter that I have received from the Establishment, although I have rendered in return for it, the money's worth.[8]

In view of the work facing him he was doubtless very relieved to be able to give up any obligation to write these additional sketches, although he did write extra ones later when Macrone published the collection.

Dickens continued in his letter:

> ... I did expect on leaving, to receive some slight written acknowledgment from the Proprietors of the Morning Chronicle of the sense they entertained of the services I had performed. I may say now, that on many occasions at a sacrifice of health, rest, and personal comfort, I have again and again, on important expresses in my zeal for the interests of the paper, done what was always before considered impossible, and what in all probability will never be accomplished again.[9]

He was thinking of his assignment to South Devon when he went to report on Lord John Russell's re-election campaign, and when with his journalist friend, Thomas Beard, he succeeded in beating *The Times* reporter back to London with a longer and more accurate report than any of his rivals.

> During the whole period of my engagement wherever there was a difficult and harassing duty to be performed—travelling at a few hours' notice hundreds of miles in the depth of winter—leaving hot and crowded rooms to write, the night through, in a close damp chaise—tearing along, and writing the most important speeches, under every possible circumstance of disadvantage and difficulty—for that duty I have been selected. And I did not think when I made great efforts to perform it, and to eclipse (as I have done, again and again) other papers with double the means, that my reward at last would be a regret that I had ever enjoyed a few weeks' rest, and a fear lest at the close of two years, I should have received six pounds six, too much![10]

This was quite a striking piece of journalism, although it was indeed a prodigious task to travel several hundred miles by night and by road, with no planes, no trains or fast cars or motorways to make such travelling easy. It was of course with particular reference to their great rival, *The Times*, that he mentions eclipsing other papers with double the means. However, the sting is perhaps in the tail of the letter:

> I have, however, the satisfaction of knowing that there is not another Newspaper Office in London where these services have not been watched and appreciated—that there is not one of my colleagues who will not cheerfully bear testimony to them—and with the respect and esteem of both Editors and reporters, I am happy to say that I can afford to

part with the thanks of the Proprietors, although I feel much hurt, and much surprised at the conduct they think proper to pursue towards me.

Depend upon it, Sir, that if you would stimulate those about you to any exertions beyond their ordinary routine of duty, and gather round you competent successors of the young men whom you will constantly find quitting a most arduous and thankless profession, as other prospects dawn upon them, this is not the way to do it.[11]

Easthope did apparently suffer a twinge of conscience and later gave a favourable review of the first number of *Bentley's Miscellany*, for which Dickens wrote 'The Public Life of Mr Tulrumble', but the novelist was far from appeased and nursed a grievance against his employers in the world of journalism for some time.

In 1865, however, when Dickens was speaking at a Newspaper Press Fund Dinner, he referred kindly to his experiences as a journalist and of the appreciation of his employers, especially of his editor, the late John Black. Among other things in his speech he said:

I have pursued the calling of a reporter under circumstances of which many of my brethren at home in England here, many of my modern successors, can form no adequate conception. I have often transcribed for the printer from my shorthand notes . . . writing on the palm of my hand, by the light of a dark lantern, in a post chaise and four, galloping through a wild country, all through the dead of night, at the then surprising rate of fifteen miles an hour . . . I have been, in my time, belated on miry by-roads, towards the small hours, in a wheelless carriage, with exhausted horses and drunken postboys, and have got back in time for publication, to be received with never forgotten compliments by the late Mr Black, coming in the broadest of Scotch, from the broadest of hearts I ever knew.[12]

On one occasion, recalling his journalistic days, Dickens said:

I have had to charge for half a dozen break downs in half a dozen times as many miles. I have had to charge for the damage of a greatcoat from the drippings of a blazing wax-candle, in writing through the smallest hours of the night in a swift-flying carriage and pair. I have had to charge for all sorts of breakages fifty times in a journey without question. I have charged for broken hats, broken luggage, broken chaises, broken harness—everything but a broken head, which is the only thing they would have grumbled to pay for . . .[13]

So Dickens broke from journalism, plunging in 1836

into the world of literature, in which he was destined to make his mark in a way he could never have visualized at that time. It was a pity that he had to break from the newspapers in this way, and one wonders whether Easthope maybe bore him a grudge for his past activities when, a year earlier, he had led a successful strike of *Morning Chronicle* reporters against the compulsory signing of an agreement. Easthope had to give way on that occasion and Dickens gained considerable kudos in Fleet Street for the way in which he had conducted the case on behalf of his colleagues against the management. Accordingly, when he finally left the newspaper, his colleagues presented him with a silver-plated goblet, which has been acquired by the Dickens House Museum and is on view at Doughty Street.

Suddenly, Dickens's friendly relationship with Macrone was rudely broken when Macrone discovered that not only had Dickens agreed to write two novels for Bentley, but was also to be editor of Bentley's magazine. Dickens may have been under the impression that Macrone had released him verbally from his obligation to write the novel *Gabriel Varden* for him. Be that as it may, Macrone decided otherwise and Harrison Ainsworth, who had been instrumental in bringing the two men together, was called upon to give judgment—much to his embarrassment.

Ainsworth, friendly with both parties, tried to steer a middle course. Whilst he felt that the publisher was entitled to the fulfilment of his contract, he also considered that the amount agreed by Macrone—£200 for the complete novel —was unreasonably small in view of Dickens's recently enhanced value. He agreed, however, that Dickens was bound by his letter and was not entitled to break his promise.

Macrone aggravated the position by advertising the novel, *Gabriel Varden*, and in the meantime was treating with Dickens for the purchase of the copyright of both the first and second series of *Sketches by Boz*. Dickens was asking £250 for the copyright of both series, but appreciating that he was in Macrone's hands in regard to the *Gabriel Varden* novel, he eventually compromised on the other point and accepted £100. Later, when the printers claimed £150 from Dickens for the cost of printing two editions of the *Sketches*, referring to him as a partner in the transaction, Dickens wrote to his solicitors stating that for the first edition of the first series, he had been paid £100; that he had never been a partner or signed any partnership agreement; that he had given up the copyright of both series to Macrone on getting back the novel agreement; that he had received about £400 but that Macrone had made over £4000.[14]

It seemed that in releasing himself from his obligation to write *Gabriel Varden*, Dickens's troubles with Macrone were settled and his literary career could forge ahead. *Pickwick* was proving a great success, Bentley had published the operetta written by Dickens—*The Village Coquettes*—and Chapman and Hall published *The Strange Gentleman*—his farce, in which John Pritt Harley, the well-known comedy actor, had been a great hit; and *Oliver Twist* had opened in *Bentley's Miscellany*. But Macrone was far from being disposed of. Taking advantage of the great popularity of *Pickwick Papers*, Macrone proposed publishing *Sketches by Boz* in monthly parts and in green wrappers, similar to those in which *Pickwick* was appearing. Dickens decided that this would be harmful to his reputation and might even affect the sale of *Pickwick*. John Forster, a literary friend of Dickens, was asked to see Macrone and point out to him that in view of the money he (Macrone) had already made out of the publication of the *Sketches*, having paid a very low figure for the copyright, perhaps he should abandon the idea.

This Macrone would not agree to, in spite of Dickens's threat to advertise that the reissue was against his wishes and that he gained no benefit by it. Macrone was once more in a strong position, and when approached with a view to selling back the copyright of the *Sketches*, he decided that he would accept nothing less than £2000. Although at this time this may have seemed a large sum of money, Chapman and Hall agreed that it was reasonable in view of the possible profits to be made and they were quite willing to put this sum up for Dickens. They considered that if the *Sketches* were to be published in monthly parts, they and the author might as well benefit by it.

By an agreement with Macrone dated 17 January 1837, the original document being now in the Widener Collection at Harvard, Chapman and Hall paid £2250: £2000 for the copyright and £250 for the remaining stock of bound volumes of the *Sketches*. Thus Macrone, after paying Dickens £100 for the copyright, immediately sold it back to him for £2000—not a bad bit of business on his part.

Now, at last, Dickens could settle down peacefully to fulfil the rest of his commitments, but he was beginning to think that he was the only one who did not make money out of his own work.

However, he was always ready to forgive and forget, and when in September 1837 he heard of Macrone's sudden death, which left his widow and children destitute after the payment of his debts, Dickens immediately devised a plan, with Harrison Ainsworth, to help them. He proposed to publish a three-volume book called *The Pic Nic Papers*, to which writers who had been associated with Macrone should be invited to contribute, the proceeds of the publication to be used to help the widow and her family. In spite of being fully occupied with his own work, Dickens, typically, threw himself wholeheartedly into the scheme. He not only contributed a story himself, but supervised all the details of printing and corresponded with a great number of literary people from whom he hoped to obtain contributions. A number responded generously, including Thomas More (a poet), Sheridan Knowles (a dramatist), Leitch Ritchie (a novelist), Harrison Ainsworth, Leigh Hunt, John Forster, Serjeant Talfourd, Allan Cunningham (a Scottish writer), Richard Bentley, H. W. Challis (pseudonym Joyce Jocund), W. H. Maxwell (an Irish soldier and writer), W. H. Harrison (a poet), G. W. Lovell (a playwright), Miss Agnes Strickland (an historian), the Hon. J. Erskine Murray (a writer) and his brother Robert Dundas Murray, also a writer, Andrew Bissett (a barrister) and many others.

An agreement with Henry Colbourn dated 10 August 1838 provided for the printing of a three-volume work and Mrs Macrone benefited to the extent of £450. Dickens himself contributed 'The Lamplighter's Story', which he adapted from a farce he had written specially for Macready, but which the actor did not consider suitable for him.

CHAPTER 4

'The Burlington Street brigand'

BENTLEY's friendly relationship with Dickens soon began
to wear thin, and for three years a niggling dispute dragged
on between them. Again and again it was patched up, only
to break out once more, until its final crisis and resolution.
Certain disagreements arose over the running of the
magazine, *Bentley's Miscellany*, and Dickens began to feel
that his editorship was being undermined. Bentley had the
right to veto any item and to introduce articles. This was
indeed necessary in the beginning when, lacking experience
in literary circles, Dickens did not always have the 'pull' to
bring in contributions. Bentley took advantage of this to
approach his own friends for contributions and sometimes
items were set up by the printer about which Dickens, as
editor, had not been consulted, and which he saw for the
first time at proof stage.

Their first serious difference arose over finance and
Bentley's desire to retain Dickens's services for an additional
five years instead of three and then, five even beyond that.
In the meantime he wanted exclusive rights to publish all
Dickens's writings apart from those already promised to
Chapman and Hall. Though, with the help and advice of
John Forster, a compromise satisfactory to Dickens was
agreed, the terms on which Bentley was to have two subsequent novels remained. The two men met for a friendly
discussion at Bentley's in Burlington Street. Dickens
suggested £600 for permission to publish three thousand
copies of a first novel—*Barnaby Rudge* (the novel he had
originally agreed to write for Macrone, under the title of
Gabriel Varden, Locksmith of London), and £700 to publish
three thousand copies of *Oliver Twist*, which Dickens
called the second novel. *Oliver Twist* was already appearing

46

in *Bentley's Miscellany* and the author was in fact expecting Bentley to accept this one story for two purposes—as a contribution to the magazine, for which he was already being paid £20 a month, and also as a 'second' novel for which a further payment was expected, notwithstanding the fact that under the agreement Bentley had the copyright. After delays, Bentley agreed the higher payments, but would not accept *Oliver Twist* as the second novel. Five instalments had already appeared in the *Miscellany*.

Dickens's first reaction was to threaten to stop writing the novel, but then an arbitrator was suggested—first Serjeant Talfourd, whom Bentley would not accept because, being Dickens's friend, he may have been biased in his favour, and then Thomas Beard. Beard was asked to meet Bentley's 'friend', who turned out to be his solicitor. At this, Dickens refused to have any further communication with Bentley, and asked that all correspondence and his salary should be sent to him through a third party. Bentley called at Doughty Street several times, only to find Dickens away. Later, Dickens sent his brother Fred to the publisher for his salary. In August Dickens wrote to Forster referring to Bentley as an 'infernal, rich, plundering, thundering old Jew,'[1] which is what Sikes called Fagin in *Oliver Twist*. Dickens also referred to Bentley in a letter as the Robber. The Rev. R. H. Barham, author of *The Ingoldsby Legends*, also mediated in Dickens's quarrels with Bentley. According to Barham's great grand-daughter, a number of letters from Dickens to Barham were burnt by her mother.[2]

It had been the custom of Bentley and Dickens to consult together to agree the set-up of each number of the magazine, but on calling at the printer's Bentley found that Dickens had sent in various papers without referring them to him. The publisher agreed most of them, but vetoed some and substituted other items. Cruikshank had meanwhile been called in as a mediator. Bentley realized that Dickens's popularity was growing fast, both with *Pickwick Papers* and *Oliver Twist*, and that it would be to his advantage to retain this young author's services. He therefore instructed Ainsworth to offer Dickens the larger sums for the two novels and to accept *Oliver Twist* as the second one. Cruikshank thought that everything had been happily arranged, but here again the affairs of the magazine were to intrude. Dickens wrote to Cruikshank, referring to sixteen pages of printed matter for the *Miscellany* which Dickens had never seen before and which Bentley, as he put it, had had the 'insolence' to send to him.[3] Following this, a letter of the same date from Dickens to Cruikshank released the latter of any further trouble in the negotiation regarding *Oliver Twist*, for he, Dickens, had ceased to be editor of the *Miscellany*.[4] On the same day, Dickens wrote to Bentley resigning from the editorship as from the end of that month.[5] Bentley felt there was nothing he could do but take legal advice. Solicitors were called in: Charles Molloy for Dickens and John Swarbreck Gregory for Bentley.

After some futile discussions and suggestions on the part of Bentley's solicitor, who seemed to have misunderstood Dickens's attitude and to assume that the problem was purely financial, the publisher realized that it would be his loss if Dickens withdrew his services. To win in court would do him no good, so he agreed to almost everything that Dickens demanded. Dickens was still not appeased and further consultations took place with a view to drawing up a new agreement. This was done on 28 September 1837. By this agreement, Dickens undertook to edit the *Miscellany* for three years (the five-year option was omitted); Bentley retained the right to veto and to introduce three items in each number. *Oliver Twist* would continue until midsummer 1838 and be published in three volumes upon its completion in the magazine, for which Dickens was to receive £500. Bentley would have the copyright for three years, after which it would revert to the author. *Barnaby Rudge* was to be published on similar terms by October 1838, but Dickens was to receive £700. Thus, the author was victorious on practically all points.[6]

The peace, however, was not of long duration, although the men met socially on several occasions. Bentley had acquired a life of Grimaldi, the celebrated clown, which he asked Dickens to revise and edit. This he agreed to do for £300 and a half share in the profits after deduction of expenses. Dickens did little writing himself on this task, dictating most of the alterations to his father, who was exceedingly proud of acting as amanuensis to his famous son.

The book sold far better than Dickens had ever imagined it would. He thought little of the work and called it 'dreary twaddle'.[7]

Very soon the editorial disputes arose anew and although Bentley, under the new agreement, had the right to introduce contributions, Dickens refused to be responsible for them. Papers Dickens selected were often never used and it soon became obvious that his control as editor hardly existed. Finally, in despair, he told Bentley to order the *Miscellany* as he liked and that he no longer cared about it. He emphasized, however, that he did not wish Captain Marryat, the American novelist whose material Bentley had used without permission, to think that he, Dickens, had pillaged his article from an American paper and advertised him as contributor. Nor would he continue any longer to accept papers which would never be used; in future he would let Bentley have his opinion of the papers sent to him and leave him to do as he pleased with them.[8]

Bentley was unwise, to say the least of it, not to appreciate that Dickens could very easily be upset on small points. This was certainly the case when Dickens discovered, on looking over an account of the *Miscellany* sales, that Bentley was making small deductions when his *Oliver* instalment fell short by a page or less. He was astonished at this meanness, and recollected that on several occasions he had made cuts in these instalments to suit the exigencies of various numbers. He also reminded Bentley that some thirty or forty pounds were due to him on account of the *Miscellany* sales and asked him if he considered it liberal to his editor to deduct half pages and count him down by the line. He suggested that the care he took and the pains he bestowed upon the tale, of which Bentley seemed to be counting the words, surely deserved a better return. Such treatment did not encourage Dickens to continue their business connection.[9] And yet letters in the following month, in which arrangements to meet were made, Bentley's offer for *The Pic Nic Papers* was mentioned, and free copies of the *Miscellany* in boards for a friend were requested, all seem to have been written in a normal friendly spirit. Obviously, these two men could not continue for long without bickering over something.

As *Oliver* neared completion, Dickens felt that to contemplate providing another serialized novel for the *Miscellany* and have *Barnaby Rudge* ready by November would be an impossible task. He therefore suggested to Bentley that *Barnaby Rudge* should follow *Oliver Twist* as the serial in the magazine. Dickens was of course already starting *Nicholas Nickleby* in monthly parts for Chapman and Hall and to attempt three stories at the same time was, he felt, beyond anyone's ability. Bentley stupidly disagreed, and continued to advertise the postponed *Barnaby Rudge*. After more protracted arguments and visits to Dickens, the publisher eventually agreed, but by January 1839 the old editorial wrangles had broken out again. Before long, Dickens was declaring to Forster that he just could not write *Barnaby*, and that there must be a six-month postponement. He referred to a net that had been wound about him, and which he must break at any cost.[10]

Of course, no one had wound a net round him—there was nothing in the terms of the contract that he had not originally agreed himself, and had been pleased to agree. The old worry was obviously in his mind, for in the same letter he referred to the immense profits which *Oliver* had realized to its publisher, and the miserable sum it had brought to him by comparison. He also contemplated the fact that he had to face the drudgery of writing another novel on the same terms. He was conscious that his books were enriching everybody connected with them but himself. 'Go it MUST,' he wrote to Forster. 'It is no fiction to say that at present I cannot write this tale.'[11]

There were undoubtedly faults on both sides. Dickens was becoming more and more bitter and disappointed at the thought of other people making money from his efforts, though it was his own fault for tying himself up at low rates, through, of course, his business inexperience. Bentley, realizing the great value of this young author, paid more and more—far above the provisions of his original agreements, but only did so after protracted delays, arguments and acrimony, and then very grudgingly. It was Bentley's nature to act in this way and he quarrelled with other writers and artists as well as Dickens. Dickens, on the other hand, who had plunged rather naively into the business of literature, was becoming more and more steeled and determined to drive a good bargain for himself as he learnt from experience.

Bentley again reluctantly agreed to a delay in the writing of *Barnaby Rudge*, provided Dickens undertook to do no work for other publishers, other than *Nicholas Nickleby*. This Dickens would not tie himself to, as he already had the book for Macrone's widow in hand, and had also been thinking of a comic Christmas book for Chapman and Hall. In the event, he did not tackle the latter, although Bentley even offered to agree to him doing that and also to double his salary to £40 a month just to allow his name to remain as editor of the *Miscellany*. His salary was eventually raised to £30.

But things had gone too far, and Dickens insisted that Harrison Ainsworth should edit the magazine. Under those conditions he would provide two further papers, give Ainsworth assistance and advice in his editorship, and not write for or conduct any other magazine until after the end of 1839.

Again Bentley agreed, but this still left the matter of *Barnaby Rudge* to be settled. Finally, yet another agreement was made, in which Dickens undertook to deliver the manuscript of *Barnaby* on 1 January 1840. He was not to undertake any other work beyond the comic Christmas book and *Nickleby* for Chapman and Hall, and the Macrone benefit book for Colbourn. Bentley agreed to pay £2000 for *Barnaby*, plus another £1000 if sales exceeded 10,000 and £1000 if sales exceeded 15,000. He was therefore paying £4000 for a book which Dickens had originally agreed to write for him for £500.[12] So *Bentley's Miscellany* was handed over to the editorship of Ainsworth, and Dickens took his farewell in a notice in the magazine, which he called 'Familiar Epistle from a Parent to a Child, Aged Two Years and Two Months'.

Nine months later, when *Barnaby* was about due, Dickens had only written two chapters and he was still very reluctant to write it. He had dropped the comic annual idea, but wrote instead a collection of papers for Chapman and Hall called *Sketches of Young Couples*, for which he was paid £200. So the war with Bentley continued. On 16 December 1839,

Dickens wrote to his solicitors, Smithson and Mitton, that in *The Morning Chronicle* he had seen Bentley's advertisement announcing that Mr Dickens's new work *Barnaby Rudge*, in three volumes, was being prepared for publication. 'I wish you if you please, without delay,' he wrote, 'formally to make known to Mr Bentley (through his agents with whom you have already corresponded) what I presume he is already perfectly well acquainted with, through Mr George Cruikshank—namely that I am not prepared to deliver the manuscript of *Barnaby Rudge* to him on the First of January.'[13]

Then followed various reasons, mainly based on the fact that Bentley had used Dickens's name improperly in advertisements. Dickens also expressed his disapproval of Bentley's practice of publishing a three-volume novel for twenty-five shillings, then, while the booksellers were fully stocked with copies, issuing it in fifteen weekly parts at a shilling each. All this, wrote the novelist, might do his reputation harm if a new novel of his was in the publisher's hands. He did not therefore intend to deliver the manuscript at the specified time. On the other hand, Bentley was entitled to cancel the agreement.

This letter of course put Bentley on the spot, and apart from cancelling the agreement, which understandably he did not want to do, his only alternative was to take legal action. Although he would undoubtedly have won such an action, it would have done him little good to ruin Dickens and destroy the goose that laid the golden eggs. In any case, winning the action would not make Dickens write the novel. As Dickens wrote to Beard, 'War to the knife and with no quarter on either side, has commenced with the Burlington Street brigand.'[14] Macready, the actor, offered his services as mediator, but Dickens declined this offer with thanks. Privately, Macready thought Dickens was in the wrong and recorded in his diary: 'He makes a contract which he considers advantageous at the time, but subsequently finding his talents more lucrative than he had supposed, he refuses to fulfil the contract.'

This was undoubtedly the truth of the case and Bentley was legally in the right, but always had to give way or lose Dickens. Unfortunately he gave way either too late, or with too grudging an air, and so lost the advantage he might have gained. Now, however, Dickens was determined to fight to the end and all Bentley had left to do was to ensure the best terms he could get. Dickens had quite made up his mind, such was his hatred of the publisher, that he could not work for him any longer.

It was not until Dickens had left Doughty Street that a final agreement was reached, satisfactory to both parties. Dickens agreed to pay Bentley £2250 for the copyright of *Oliver Twist* and the stock of 1002 copies. Chapman and Hall advanced this sum for Dickens and it was agreed that it would be deducted from the purchase price of the copyright of *Barnaby Rudge*, for which the publishers were willing to pay £3000.[15]

In fairness, it must be conceded that both Macrone and Bentley took the risk with their money of backing a young author whose abilities were only just beginning to emerge. Because the popularity of Dickens and therefore his value advanced so rapidly, the young novelist maybe had a grievance with regard to being underpaid, but he had no legal right to break his contract for that reason, and was fortunate in being able to extricate himself from the burdensome task of giving brilliant value at hack rates. He had only himself to thank for his dilemmas, but then who could have foreseen, least of all Dickens himself, his extraordinary rise in the literary world?

CHAPTER 5

Dining at Doughty Street

THE first room visitors to the Dickens House Museum enter today, on the left of the entrance hall, is the dining-room—not all that large, but impressive, with its semi-circular end and doors curved to fit into the symmetry of the room. The two doors, one an entrance from the hall, the other opening into a shallow cupboard, immediately catch the attention of the visitor. One would imagine that these doors and the shape of the room would have attracted the notice of guests dining at Doughty Street, especially on the first occasion, and maybe were an early topic of conversation when guests gathered round the long mahogany table to dine. Standing in this room, one can imagine their enthusiastic young host making his guests welcome and carrying on a bright conversation as he expertly carved the joint.

The number dining usually varied between eight and ten. The room would have been rather crowded with more people. Larger parties would be accommodated later in the next house, where the rooms were much larger, and as Catherine recorded in her cookery book, '*What Shall We Have For Dinner?*', a typical menu for eight or ten might have been:

Oyster Soup   *Vermicelli Soup*
Cods' Heads   *Smelts*   *Fried Whitings*
Saddle of Mutton   *Curried Oysters*
Veal Olives
Tongue   *Fricassée Chicken*
Lobster Salad
Two Boiled Fowls   *Oyster Sauce*
Two Wild Ducks   *Two Pheasants*
Lemon Pudding   *Jelly*   *Tart*

In another menu for the same number of people Kate provided Roast Turkey, Haunch of Mutton, Pigeon Pie, Boiled Turkeys, Two Woodcocks, Hare and Four Snipes.[1] It seems rather doubtful whether she had brought her catering up to that standard at Doughty Street. According to letters written by Dickens they appear to have lived mostly on chops !

Dining time tended to become later as the century advanced, possibly because of the introduction of luncheon and afternoon tea. At the beginning of the sixteenth century for example, dinner was at 11 a.m.; 150 years later it had advanced to 1 p.m. and by the beginning of the eighteenth century, to 2 p.m. By mid-eighteenth century dinner was at 4 p.m.,[2] and so to Dickens's time when he usually dined about 5 or 5.30 p.m. Thackeray dined later at 6 p.m. By 1865, when *Our Mutual Friend* was written, dinner was later still. It will be remembered that Mr Podsnap's maxim was:

> The world got up at eight,
> shaved close at a quarter past,
> breakfasted at nine,
> went to the City at ten,
> came home at half-past four,
> and dined at seven.

One of the very early letters Dickens wrote from Doughty Street was to his new acquaintance, John Forster, who became his life-long friend and biographer, and whom he first met at Ainsworth's home in Kensal Lodge, the previous Christmas. In the letter, he says they only called upon him a second time in the hope of getting him to dine with them, and were disappointed not to find him. After referring to his 'pleasant occupation of moving', Dickens pointed out that he was engaged to the *Pickwick* publishers for a dinner in honour of that hero, due to take place the next day. Much as he would have preferred to dine with Forster, he was unable to accept his invitation.[3]

Another early diner at Doughty Street was a reporter named John Ross. In a letter to Thomas Beard, Dickens told him that John Ross was dining with them on Saturday, and hoped that he would do likewise at 5 o'clock.[4] On another occasion when Beard was invited to dine, he apparently had a black eye, because Dickens says 'you needn't mind your eye', pointing out that they will be alone. He is, however, rather curious as to how Beard came by it: 'Did you take it naturally or bacchanalially?'[5]

Charles Ross, Parliamentary Reporter on *The Times* for over sixty years, and later chief of its parliamentary staff,[6] was known to Dickens in the gallery of the House of Commons and also when, for the short period 1837–9, Ross was on the staff of *The Morning Chronicle*. He had been a guest of Dickens in Fitzroy Street and had been party to a sing-song there one evening. John, his brother, was also a *Times* reporter, and Janet, their sister, was Dickens's aunt by marriage. She painted his earliest known portrait, a miniature, now on view in the Doughty Street Museum, and also a miniature portrait of Frederick Dickens, Dickens's brother.

Ralph Nickleby, calling on his sister-in-law and her family, Nicholas and Kate, in their lodgings in the Strand, stops at a private door about half-way down that crowded thoroughfare:

> A miniature painter lived there, for there was a large gilt frame screwed upon the street door, in which were displayed, upon a black velvet ground, two portraits of naval dress coats with faces looking out of them, and telescopes attached; one of a young gentleman in a very vermilion uniform, flourishing a sabre; and one of a literary character with a high forehead, a pen and ink, six books and curtain. There was, moreover, a touching representation of a young lady reading a manuscript in an unfathomable forest, and a charming whole length of a large-headed little boy, sitting on a stool with his legs foreshortened to the size of salt spoons. Besides these works of art, there were a great many heads of old ladies and gentlemen smirking at each other out of blue and green skies, and an elegantly written card of terms with an embossed border.[7]

One wonders whether Janet Ross spotted this bit of fun at her expense. Although she may have inspired the portrait of Miss La Creevy in *Nicholas Nickleby*, who is a pleasant character, Dickens described her as 'the wearer of the yellow head-dress, who had a gown to correspond, and was of much the same colour herself . . . a mincing young lady of fifty . . .'; it is doubtful whether Janet Ross would have felt very flattered.

Dickens was said to have been in love with another of the Ross sisters, Georgina, and indeed to have been engaged to her. Georgina was nine years older than Dickens and the match was not encouraged by her father, who apparently decided that the young man was too worldly to make a good husband for his daughter. She never married.[8] He wrote in her album an early version of 'The Ivy Green', which he later used in *Pickwick Papers*, where it is recited by the old clergyman during Mr Pickwick's first visit to Manor Farm, Dingley Dell:

> Oh, a dainty plant is the Ivy green,
> That creepeth o'er ruins old!
> Of right choice food his meals I ween,
> In his cell so lone and cold.
> The wall must be crumbled, the stone decayed,
> To pleasure his dainty whim;
> And the mouldering dust that years have made
> Is a merry meal for him.
>   Creeping where no life is seen,
>   A rare old plant is the Ivy green.[9]

A somewhat melancholy verse to write in a young lady's album!

Thomas Beard, a journalist sometimes referred to as 'Dickens's oldest friend', was best man at his wedding and godfather to his eldest son, Charley. It was Beard who obtained a reporting post for Dickens on *The Morning Chronicle* in 1834, and who was his companion on many of his most important reporting assignments. He helped Dickens with small loans of a pound or two in the lean days, and later Dickens reciprocated by helping him in a similar manner.[10] The earliest guests of the Dickens family at Doughty Street, therefore, apart from parents and a few relations, were quite understandably newspaper friends, for up to that time Dickens had become quite a well-known figure and indeed a bright star in the newspaper world.

On 20 April, soon after Dickens moved into Doughty Street, Richard Bentley, for whom he was editor, was invited there for coffee and to discuss the proposed contents of the next number of the *Miscellany*. He was not asked to dine on that occasion and Dickens referred to his position as being 'head over ears with Oliver'.[11] Bentley was invited to dine, however, nine days later, when George Hogarth, Dickens's father-in-law, and Cruikshank were coming. 'A little music in the evening' was promised. Dickens's brother Fred was the bearer of this letter; in fact, he seemed to fill the post of messenger on many occasions.[12]

George Cruikshank was possibly the most famous illustrator of his day, and Dickens, an unknown writer of twenty-four, was very fortunate to have this established artist illustrating his *Sketches by Boz* and his second novel, *Oliver Twist*.

Before Dickens ever met him, George Hogarth had been music critic for the *Evening Chronicle*; he was eventually invited to be editor, and it was in that capacity that he asked Dickens, who had been contributing short sketches and stories to several magazines without payment, to write some London street sketches for the evening paper. For these Dickens had received an extra 2 guineas a week to add to his salary of 5 guineas for his work as Parliamentary Reporter. (This was the beginning of the collection which became known as *Sketches by Boz*.) Dickens, asked home by Hogarth to meet his family, had courted the eldest daughter, Catherine, and married her. Hogarth, prior to his work on the London newspaper, had been Writer to *The Signet* in Edinburgh and a legal practitioner before the Court of Session. He was a friend of Sir Walter Scott and one of his advisers. His sister had married James Ballantyne, with whom his brother ran a printing business in which Scott was a partner. Hogarth married a daughter of George Thomson, a friend of Robert Burns. Dickens therefore gained several Scottish connections when he married Catherine Hogarth.

Richard Bentley had dissolved his partnership with Colbourn, who had retained their best authors. Bentley, realizing the potential of this rising young author Dickens, had asked him to write a novel for him, but had been forestalled by Macrone. The disputes and difficulties that arose between these publishers and Dickens have been described in the two preceding chapters.

Many years later Bentley described his first evening at
Doughty Street, in April 1837: 'Dinner in Doughty
Street. I the only stranger. Mr Dickens, Sen., Mr Hogarth,
Miss Dickens, the Misses Hogarth.' (Possibly Bentley
meant Mrs, not Miss Dickens.) Bentley described it as a
right merry entertainment. Dickens apparently sang two or
three songs, including the patter song, 'The Dog's Meat
Man', and gave sundry imitations of famous actors of the
day. No small wonder that Mary worshipped her talented
and lively brother-in-law! When Bentley rose to leave at
about midnight Dickens pressed him to take another glass
of brandy from the hand of Mary Hogarth, which the
visitor found it difficult to refuse. Then he referred to
'the following Thursday's' (he meant Saturday's) visit to the
theatre and Mary dying in Dickens's arms 'of a hysterical
fit'. How he arrived at this description of the cause of
Mary's death is unknown. He possibly gained this impression from verbal accounts given to him of her symptoms.[13]

Apart from Mary's funeral and the melancholy partaking
of refreshments on returning from that sad event, the
dining-room at Doughty Street was without guests for a
time, while Dickens and his wife recovered from their
shock at Hampstead. Whether Fred remained at Doughty
Street is not clear, but if he did, the house must have seemed
a very lonely and sad one after all the laughter and happiness
that had formerly filled it. Although Charles and Kate were
at Hampstead until the end of May, he returned most
evenings to Doughty Street, from which address he wrote to
Bentley for £30 in respect of their monthly settlement, as
he had 'various calls'[14] upon him.

Early in June, when they had returned to Doughty
Street from Collins's Farm, he wrote to Mrs Hogarth most
affectionately, very concerned for her health and wanting to
know all that had happened during their absence. He also
wanted to see Mr and Mrs Thomson and hoped they would
dine at 48 on the next day.[15] George Thomson was Kate's
maternal grandfather.[16]

In June, Harrison Ainsworth, the historical novelist,
was asked to dine, after a visit to Newgate Prison,[17] but he
excused himself both from the prison visit and the dinner
following because of business commitments. Dickens

suggested in a letter to Forster, referring to this cancellation, that the 'business' might have been 'Mrs Touchitt's wrath'. Mrs Touchet, widow of Ainsworth's cousin, and her sister Anne looked after the novelist at Kensal Lodge, after he was separated from his wife, and being a rather 'strong minded and sharp tongued character', evidently ruled him and his household.[18] Writing to Forster some days later, Dickens said: 'I am glad I was right about Ainsworth. Mrs Touchitt for ever.'[19]

Harrison Ainsworth was Dickens's close friend at the beginning of the young novelist's career, gave him encouragement, introduced him to publishers and illustrators and was, with John Forster, his constant companion. Together, these three friends formed themselves into what they called the Cerberus Club and had special goblets made etched with a three-headed emblem. Strange to say, there were five of these goblets, which appeared in the sale at Gad's Hill after the death of Dickens, one lot of two and another of three. It seems possible that extra ones were made and that there were originally six, one of which may have been broken.

In the first few years of their friendship, Ainsworth was often with Dickens and Forster. They dined at each other's houses and went on horse-riding jaunts. The other two would pick up Ainsworth at his house, Kensal Lodge, and ride by Twyford Abbey and the clear, winding River Brent to Perivale and Greenford, Ruislip, Stanmore and Harrow. At other times they would ride across Oak Common to Acton, stopping for a few moments at Berrymead Priory, greeting Bulwer Lytton, then through the narrow High Street of Acton, past Fordhook, Fielding's home, across the parks and long village green at Ealing, to Chiswick, Shepherd's Bush and Wood Lane—so home again.[20] Or another time, when the riding party was joined by Talfourd, the route was via Richmond and Twickenham, through the Park, out at Knightsbridge and over Barnes Common—described as a beautiful ride.[21]

Thomas Noon Talfourd, judge, essayist and dramatist, was associated with the case *Norton v. Melbourne*, on which Dickens reported, and many details of which he used in *Bardell v. Pickwick*. Talfourd was watched by the young reporter in the House of Commons when defending the cause of copyright. Throughout his career Dickens suffered at the hands of plagiarists. He was persuaded by Talfourd to take action against a firm of publishers who had produced a blatant copy of *A Christmas Carol*. Dickens won his case easily, even without Talfourd delivering his carefully prepared speech for the prosecution. Talfourd, amiable, gentle, and sweet-tempered, was thought to be the original of the delightful Tommy Traddles in *David Copperfield*.[22]

Ainsworth attended all the early celebration dinners to mark the completion of various books up to *Dombey and Son*, and Dickens attended the dinner to mark the completion of Ainsworth's *Tower of London*. It was no doubt because of the great popularity of Ainsworth's highwayman stories that in the part of *Pickwick* written at Doughty Street Dickens made Sam Weller sing 'Bold Turpin vunce on Hounslow Heath', and it was also significant that Turpin's robber colleague was named Sikes.

> Bold Turpin vunce, on Hounslow Heath,
> His bold mare Bess bestrode—er;
> Ven there he see'd the Bishop's coach
> A-coming along the road—er.
> So he gallops close to the 'orse's legs,
> And he claps his head vithin;
> And the Bishop says, 'Sure as eggs is eggs,
> This here's the bold Turpin!'[23]

(It was pointed out that the monosyllable at the end of the second and fourth lines not only enables the singer to take breath at those points, but greatly assists the metre.)

Later, Ainsworth and Dickens seem to have drifted apart and seldom saw each other, though it is not known whether there was any quarrel. It was a pity, because the older novelist was undoubtedly a valued friend, and a frequent guest in the dining-room at Doughty Street at the beginning of Dickens's career.

At one time Dickens had to excuse himself from an appointment with Ainsworth, because he was dining out at Greenwich with the Literary Fund Club,[24] after attending his sister Letitia's wedding to Henry Austin at St George's, Bloomsbury.

In June 1837, Macready and Harley both dined at
Doughty Street: the theatre was appearing in the dining-
room. What a thrill it must have been for Dickens to have
such famous theatrical personalities as friends, visiting his
home! He really loved the theatre, and all connected with
it.[25]

William Charles Macready was the leading actor-
manager of his day. He had been introduced to Dickens by
Forster and his friendship was greatly valued by the young
novelist.[26] John Pritt Harley was leading comedian at St
James's Theatre and also appeared with Macready at
Covent Garden Theatre. He was celebrated for his
Shakespearean clowns, and also appeared in the pieces
written by Dickens—*The Strange Gentleman*, in which he
scored a great success, and *Is She His Wife?* When Dickens
published his operetta, *The Village Coquettes*, it was dedicated
to Harley.[27]

Forster was frequently being invited to dine—not only on
social occasions, but sometimes as a close friend: for
example, when Dickens was at home with a cold and his
wife was going out, he wrote to ask him over ('My missis is
going out to dinner . . .'). Again he was invited to enjoy the
oft-repeated menu—'arter a lamb chop',[28] or 'Can you
come and take a cutlet with us to-day at 5? Let me know
and we'll add a bit of fish.'[29] Sometimes a change is offered:
' "*Dine*" with us by all means. We have a piece of roast
beef, and there being only you, I, Kate and Frederick . . . a
pleasant little tête à tête of four.'[30] At other times, only a
short note was sent, such as—'I shall expect you—chops
await you',[31] or again, 'unless you chop with me at 5 . . .'[32]
Occasionally the time of dining was changed for some special
purpose as

'My man's an Ass. We dine

at 4

4 !

4 ! !

4 ! ! !

4 ! ! ! ![33]

On one occasion, Forster was offered Henry, Dickens's
manservant, as messenger,[34] and a day or so later when
again being invited to dinner, Henry had apparently been

dismissed for impudence to the 'Missis' and Dickens was asking Forster for a steady man to replace him.[35] Henry was eventually replaced by Topping, a groom. About this time Dickens bought a vehicle for £125 from Eldridge and Hay, coachbuilders of 71 Great Queen Street, Lincoln's Inn Fields.[36] On yet another occasion Forster was reminded that he was to be at Doughty Street at five, to meet 'Bankes', Harley and half a dozen people.[37]

Perceval Weldon Banks (not spelt with an 'e' as by Dickens) was an Irish barrister and writer, and editor of *Fraser's Literary Chronicle*.[38] After Forster, Ainsworth and Harley were the guests most frequently invited to dine at Doughty Street.

One invitation to Harley was expressed by Dickens in verse:

Two aunts and two uncles, a sister and brother
Dine with us next Thursday; will you make another?[39]

Or at another time: 'George Cruikshank and his wife, and Burnett and his'n dine with us on Wednesday. Will you please me by joining us?'[40] Harley was invited to Charley's birthday and Mary's christening, held on the same day, at which a few friends were to be present.[41] Sometimes it was earlier, maybe because of getting to the theatre—'Can you take a family dinner with me, and a man called Thackeray, whom perhaps you know; no one else.'[42]

Harley was of course often occupied at the theatre and he was invited to join the party afterwards, when he had done 'Trinculizing' on the tempestuous seas at Covent Garden (he was playing the part of Trinculo in *The Tempest*). Occasionally there were larger parties, as on Dickens's twenty-seventh birthday—Ainsworth, Forster, Tom Mitton, Browne, Mother and Father, Fanny, Henry Burnett, Laman Blanchard, Leigh Hunt, Angus Fletcher, Mr and Mrs Dickens and Harley.[43] That made it fourteen, which must have been a tight squeeze in the dining-room.

Ainsworth is warned that they are dining at four, presumably because Dickens had a private box at Covent Garden, with Procter and Forster.[44] (Bryan Waller Procter was a lawyer who wrote under the name of Barry Cornwall.) From his letters it is clear that Dickens attended the theatre many times whilst living at Doughty Street.

Dickens gave an informal 'semi-business' dinner to celebrate the completion of *Pickwick Papers*, on 18 November 1837, at Dejex's, the Prince of Wales, No. 1 Leicester Place, Leicester Square, and invitations were sent to a number of friends and business associates—Thomas Hill, a retired drysalter and book collector, Charles Hicks, foreman printer of Bradbury and Evans, who were printers to Chapman and Hall, William Jerdan, journalist and editor of *The Literary Gazette*, W. C. Macready, Samuel Lover— miniature painter, song writer, novelist and dramatist, George Cruikshank, John Forster and Browne ('Phiz'), Dickens's illustrator.

Soon after it was Christmas, their first to be spent at Doughty Street, and no doubt a great deal of work went into providing the usual Christmas fare. To start with, the puddings had to be prepared, with the customary family stirrings, and cooked in the wash-house copper. The copper is still there, in the basement of No. 48. These coppers, used for boiling clothes, were mounted in a bricked-up space in the corner over a fire, and contained a large metal bowl, with a wooden lid. The clothes were stirred round and round with a wooden stick. Such sticks were symbolical weapons, with which irate wives would subdue their husbands, or, as in the case of Punch and Judy, with which the husband would menace his wife. The basic principle of stirring washing with a stick is of course common to many modern washing machines.

The coppers posed problems for the housewife, because the chimneys or flues from the fire were narrow and twisted, which made it difficult for the sweep to push his long brush up to clean it. One housewife of more than usual ingenuity hit upon the plan of purchasing a halfpennyworth of gunpowder, screwing it up in a newspaper and lighting it in the grate of the copper. The resultant 'whooosh' with which gunpowder burns when ignited—as demonstrated by various fireworks—was supposed to propel it up the narrow chimney and bring down the soot, which could then be conveniently swept up. Unfortunately, gunpowder has other attributes and, as also evidenced in fireworks, when confined into a tight space does not burn with a 'whooosh', but explodes with a loud and violent bang—which would happen when the housewife had screwed the gunpowder up too tightly in the newspaper; the result was a wrecked copper.

To return to the puddings: once a year, the clothes coppers were scoured out and used for boiling the puddings for Christmas and the New Year. Extra ones were cooked, to be stored on larder shelves for use during the year on various anniversaries. The Christmas puddings were so impregnated with spirits, old ale and spices that they would easily keep, as indeed they did throughout the year. It has been pointed out to me that puddings were often made purposely a year in advance because they improved with keeping.

The puddings were contained in a cloth—not in basins—as immortalized in the famous little story, *A Christmas Carol*, written by Dickens four years after he left Doughty Street.

> 'Every idiot who goes about with "Merry Christmas" on his lips should be boiled with his own pudding and buried with a stake of holly through his heart. He should!'

So said Ebenezer Scrooge, the old miser, to which his jovial nephew could only plead—'Uncle!' At a far happier moment, 'the two young Cratchits hustled Tiny Tim, and bore him off into the wash-house that he might hear the pudding singing in the copper'.

What a happy thought! There was only one pudding on that occasion, Bob Cratchit's Christmas Day, and it was a small one for a large family at that. He could not afford more on his meagre salary of fifteen shillings a week. Dickens's weekly wage at the blacking warehouse was only six, and so was mine when I started as office boy in a large draper's in Oxford Street in 1912!

After the goose:

> Mrs Cratchit left the room alone—too nervous to bear witnesses—to take the pudding up and bring it in. Suppose it should not be done enough! Suppose it should break in the turning out! Suppose somebody should have got over the wall of the back-yard, and stolen it, while they were merry with the goose—a supposition at which the two young Cratchits became livid! All sorts of horrors were supposed.
>
> Hallo! A great deal of steam! The pudding was out of the copper. A smell like washing day! That was the cloth. A smell like an eating-

house and a pastry cook's next door to each other, with a laundress's next door to that! That was the pudding! In half a minute Mrs Cratchit entered—flushed, but smiling proudly—with the pudding, like a speckled cannon-ball, so hard and firm, blazing in half of half-a-quartern of lighted brandy, and bedight with Christmas holly stuck into the top.[45]

A little poetic licence perhaps—a blazing pudding with holly in the top—I never managed that myself! But what a Christmas picture! How many times has that scene been read and acted on stage and screen, and many a budding actor or actress has had his or her part on an amateur stage as one of the Cratchit family?

Possibly these pen pictures were more reminiscent of the Camden Town house, in which Dickens lived as a boy, for the wash-house at Doughty Street is down in the basement, away from the dining-room; but these impressions were building up into the material of that remarkable little Christmas story, as with the glowing descriptions of the Christmas shops. A composite picture, accumulated over the years maybe, it included some of the shops around Doughty Street, in Lambs Conduit Street, in the markets— Leather Lane and Farringdon Street, and even around Smithfield, where no doubt, before they were well enough off to have the shopping done for them, Kate must have looked for food bargains.

The poulterer's shops were still half open, and the fruiterers' were radiant in their glory. There were great, round, pot-bellied baskets of chestnuts, shaped like the waistcoats of jolly old gentlemen, lolling at the doors, and tumbling out into the street in their apoplectic opulence. There were ruddy, brown-faced, broad-girthed Spanish Onions, shining in the fatness of their growth like Spanish Friars, and winking from their shelves in wanton slyness at the girls as they went by, and glanced demurely at the hung-up mistletoe. There were pears and apples, clustered high in blooming pyramids; there were bunches of grapes, made in the shopkeepers' benevolence to dangle from conspicuous hooks, that people's mouths might water gratis as they passed; there were piles of filberts, mossy and brown, recalling in their fragrance, ancient walks among the woods, and pleasant shufflings ankle deep through withered leaves; there were Norfolk Biffins, squab and swarthy, setting off the yellow of the oranges and lemons, and in the great compactness of their juicy persons, urgently entreating and beseeching to be carried home in paper bags and eaten after dinner. The very gold and silver fish, set forth among these choice fruits in a bowl, though members of a dull and stagnant-blooded race, appeared to know that there was something going on; and, to a fish, went gasping round and round their little world in slow and passionless excitement.[46]

Did Dickens ever keep a bowl of goldfish, one wonders? Possibly his children did.

Innumerable friends, acquaintances, business colleagues and some famous names appear on that dining list as Dickens rapidly built up his position in the literary world during those three years at Doughty Street. He was beginning to be accepted into more serious literary circles and had been a guest at the literary breakfasts given by Samuel Rogers. Kate could not aspire to enter such circles and although Rogers was always gracious to her when he called at Doughty Street, she never attended such functions,[47] where she would undoubtedly have been at sea in the conversation.

The young novelist was also accepted into a more aristocratic stratum of society and had been introduced to Count D'Orsay, by Talfourd. The Count D'Orsay was a French artist who came to England in 1821 and later joined the Countess of Blessington, authoress, in establishing a fashionable côterie in London. He lived upon his wits and a story told about him illustrates his philosophy. Being in debt, he borrowed £10 from a major. Next day he handed £750 to the major, saying 'It is yours. I gambled with your £10 last night and won this. It is yours most justly, for if I had lost I should never have repaid the £10.'[48]

He drew two portraits of Dickens which are exhibited in the Museum at Doughty Street. Count D'Orsay exercised a great influence on Dickens's dress. Dickens's great partiality to colourful and flamboyant waistcoats, which so astonished America on his first visit to the States, no doubt had its origin in this friendship. From this introduction Dickens was admitted to the famous literary salons of Lady Holland and Lady Blessington at Gore House, where he met Walter Savage Landor, later to become Mr Boythorn in *Bleak House.*

Among other close friends who dined at Doughty Street was Thomas Mitton, a solicitor who was invited to partake of Smithson's (his partner's) turkey at 5 o'clock,[49] and the following month is asked to superintend the purchase of a horse, for which five and forty guineas was to be offered, and to dine afterwards at five.[50] It is thought that the Dickens and Mitton families may have been neighbours in Camden Town. Mitton's sister, Mary Ann, claimed that she knew Dickens when he was a boy and he used to visit her parents at Manor Farm, Sunbury, which must have been when he was eighteen. She claimed also that she was the original of Little Dorrit and that it was a nickname given to her by Dickens long before he wrote the book of that title.[51] Did he also get the name of Manor Farm, Dingley Dell (in *Pickwick*) from this farm at Sunbury? There were of course numerous Manor Farms in those days.

Early in 1838, Dickens wrote that 'Little Hall and his little wife and his big partner are going to dine here on Saturday next, at half past five'. He asks Ainsworth to join them to talk about his proposed book for Macrone, *The Lions of London*. It was never written.[52]

Little Hall and his big partner were the publishers Chapman and Hall, and Mr and Mrs Hall were thought to be the originals of Mr and Mrs Chirrup, the Nice Little Couple in *Sketches of Young Couples*, written in 1840.

> Mr and Mrs Chirrup are the nice little couple in question. Mr Chirrup has the smartness and something of the brisk, quick manner of a small bird. Mrs Chirrup is the prettiest of all little women, and has the prettiest little figure conceivable. She has the neatest little foot, and the softest little voice, and the pleasantest little smile, and the tidiest little curls, and the brightest little eyes, and the quietest little manner, and is, in short, altogether one of the most engaging of all little women, dead or alive.

An interesting and effective little study in superlatives and diminutives. Sometimes it was well to be known by Dickens—it all depended upon the character for which he cast you in his books.

Dickens was said by his daughter to be a wonderfully neat and rapid carver, and in his very first story he refers to Mr Octavius Budden 'cutting or rather maiming the ham in utter violation of all established rules', to the horror of his host, Mr Augustus Minns. Mrs Chirrup is far different, and it is worth recalling this interesting account of carving:

But if there be one brand of housekeeping in which she excels to an utterly and unparalleled and unprecedented extent, it is in the important one of carving. A roast goose is universally allowed to be the great stumbling-block in the way of young aspirants to perfection in this department of science; many promising carvers, beginning with legs of mutton, and preserving a good reputation through fillets of veal, sirloins of beef, quarters of lamb, fowls and even ducks, have sunk before a roast goose, and lost cast and character for ever. To Mrs Chirrup the resolving of a goose into its smallest component parts is a pleasant pastime —a practical joke—a thing to be done in a minute or so, without the smallest interruption to the conversation of the time. No handing the dish over to an unfortunate man upon her right or left, no wild sharpening of the knife, no hacking and sawing at an unruly joint, no noise, no splash, no heat, no leaving off in despair; all is confidence and cheerfulness. The dish is set upon the table, the cover is removed; for an instant, and only an instant, you observe that Mrs Chirrup's attention is distracted; she smiles, but heareth not. You proceed with your story; meanwhile the glittering knife is slowly upraised, both Mrs Chirrup's wrists are slightly but not ungracefully agitated, she compresses her lips for an instant, then breaks into a smile, and all is over. The legs of the bird slide gently down into a pool of gravy, the wings seem to melt from the body, the breast separates into a row of juicy slices, the smaller and more complicated parts of his anatomy are perfectly developed, a cavern of stuffing is revealed, and the goose is gone![53]

It was Hall who sold Dickens a copy of *The Monthly Magazine*, in which his first story appeared—'A Dinner at Poplar Walk'. When he saw his first literary effort 'in all the glory of print', the author had to hide his tears of pride and joy, in the kindly shadows of Westminster Hall. It was almost like a premonition of all the great success to come. It was Hall who called upon him at Furnival's Inn to commission the writing of *Pickwick Papers*. Dickens must have had a very soft spot for this little man and no doubt made him very welcome at Doughty Street. In writing to Ainsworth to join the party Dickens told him that George and *his* stout lady were coming, which was George Cruikshank and his wife.

The only wife who does not seem to be recorded as dining there is Mrs Hablot K. Browne, the illustrator's wife. The Brownes had quite a considerable family and one would have thought that they and the Dickens family would have joined in various celebrations. Browne, however, was a very retiring man and not really comfortable in company, so maybe this had something to do with it. Mrs Browne was also much occupied with household affairs, and the upbringing of the youngest baby. One of the sons, in a book about his father and Dickens, says they went to live in Croydon for his mother's health and they often joined with another family of eighteen children, living at the other end of the town, to prevent them feeling lonely! Croydon was also looked upon as being in the country and considered quite a journey from London in those days. The result of their move, says Edgar Browne, was to separate his (Edgar's) father from his artistic friends.[54]

Although it is not always recorded in his letters, no doubt Dickens's parents were often dining at Doughty Street, and very proud John Dickens must have been of his son, making his way so successfully in the world. When John Dickens was acting as amanuensis to his son in the editing of *The Memoirs of Grimaldi*, no doubt he was often there for meals. On one occasion Dickens expressed his regret to Talfourd that he could not see him, because his father had come to dine.[55] On another occasion he invited his father to dine and go to the Adelphi.[56]

Many other names appear at more or less regular intervals: Thomas Hill, a rich book-collector of Sydenham, was invited to dine one evening at half past five punctually;[57] Dr Quin, first homeopathic physician in England and founder in 1850 of the Homeopathic Hospital, was invited to Mary's christening;[58] John Noble is thanked for the Highland whisky, which Dickens says he is trying that night;[59] possibly whisky was not one of his more usual drinks. John Noble lived at 90 Gloucester Place, Portman Square, and probably met Dickens at the Antiquaries Club. Dickens wrote in Miss Noble's album the words of the first verse of 'Autumn Leaves', a song in *The Village Coquettes*, his operetta.[60] He certainly seemed to write some very melancholy verses in the albums of his lady friends!

> Autumn leaves, autumn leaves, lie strewn around me here;
> Autumn leaves, autumn leaves, how sad, how cold, how drear!

How like the hopes of childhood days,
Thick clustering on the bough !
How like those hopes is their decay,—
How faded are they now !

Angus Fletcher, a Scottish sculptor, was invited to join
'divers aunts and uncles' at dinner at 6 o'clock, which
seems to be the first reference in the letters to a later dining
time.[61] Fletcher made a bust of Dickens, which is now on
view in the morning room in Doughty Street. He was a
somewhat boisterous character, sometimes rather an embarrassment in public. He was introduced to Dickens by
Macrone and the novelist nicknamed him 'Kindheart'. He
accompanied Dickens on his tour in the Highlands of
Scotland.

Beard's invitation to dine was for an earlier time (half
past four) on a Sunday, and he was asked to give his opinion
of the 'new turn out'. This was the light vehicle Dickens
had just purchased. In his letter Dickens points out that he
is haunted with his disgusting idea of Browne's table-lamp
glass being like the 'pan of a tavern water closet'.[62]

To William Longman Dickens writes: 'Family dinner at
home—uncles, aunts, brothers, sisters, cousins—an annual
gathering.'[63] Longman was the son of the publisher T. N.
Longman and the author of travel and historical books.[64]

By 1839, if not earlier, Dickens had met Miss Burdett
Coutts and was corresponding with her.[65] She probably
did not dine with him at Doughty Street. He later became
her secretary and adviser for the carrying out of her many
charitable projects. She was the daughter of Thomas Coutts,
the banker, and later became the Baroness Burdett Coutts
and a millionairess.

Clarkson Stanfield was another artist known to Dickens
in the Doughty Street days; he had first met him at Covent
Garden Theatre and later became his very close friend.
Stanfield was a marine and landscape Royal Academy
painter, who served in the Navy and painted scenery for
Dickens's amateur theatrical productions,[66] *The Lighthouse*
and *The Frozen Deep*. He was ill in bed at his home in
Hampstead when Dickens called on him and asked him to
paint the scenery for *The Lighthouse*. Apparently the effort

made him feel better. Dickens could be quite a demanding friend.

Dickens wrote with great gusto and obvious enjoyment about meals, yet according to his sister-in-law, Georgina Hogarth, he was the most abstemious of men. Although he appeared to revel in these gargantuan feasts, what he really enjoyed was greeting his guests through the steam of the 'seething bowls of punch'[67] which he had prepared, and indeed getting pleasure from the fruits of his thought and efforts. He delighted in the planning of meals. It was possibly to the meals in his larger, more luxurious house at 1 Devonshire Terrace that these literary feasts owe most, and yet much of the foundation must have been laid for them earlier in Doughty Street; and of course, all the vast programme of eating and drinking in *Pickwick* and *Nickleby* was planned in the earlier days. In *Pickwick Papers* alone, there are some 25 breakfasts, 32 dinners, 10 lunches, 10 teas, 8 suppers and 65 light snacks, also 250 occasions on which various drinks are taken.

Entries in his bank book against Ellis and Son (wine merchants) indicate Dickens's love of entertaining, in which bent he was following his father, except that he paid his wine merchants' bills—John Dickens left someone else to pay them!

It was not until Dickens had left Doughty Street and was staying in France that he sent a recipe for brewing of punch to 'Mrs. F.' It is not clear who the lady is, but I can certainly guarantee the excellence of this punch if the directions are carefully followed. This will be vouched for, I am sure, by Mr Cedric Dickens, who is an expert compounder of this delightful drink and in that respect can rival the ability of his great-grandfather. The recipe for three pints of punch is:

Peel into a very strong common basin (which may be broken in case of accident, without damage to the owner's peace or pocket) the rinds of three lemons, cut very thin and with as little as possible of the white coating between the peel and the fruit, attached. Add a double handfull of lump sugar (good measure), a pint of good old rum, and a large wine-glass of brandy—if it be not a large claret glass, say two. Set this on fire, by filling a warm silver spoon with the spirit, lighting the contents at a wax taper, and pouring them gently in. Let it burn three or four minutes at least, stirring it from time to time. Then extinguish it by covering the basin with a tray, which will immediately put out the flame. Then squeeze in the juice of the three lemons, and add a quart of *boiling* water. Stir the whole well, cover it up for five minutes, and stir again.

At this crisis (having skimmed off the lemon pips with a spoon) you may taste. If not sweet enough, add sugar to your liking, but observe that it will be a *little* sweeter presently. Pour the whole into a jug, tie a leather or coarse cloth over the top, so as to exclude the air completely, and stand it in a hot oven ten minutes, or on a hot stove one quarter of an hour. Keep it until it comes to table in a warm place near the fire, but not too hot. If it be intended to stand three or four hours, take half the lemon peel out, or it will acquire a bitter taste. The same punch allowed to grow cool by degrees, and then iced, is delicious.[68]

Warning should be given perhaps about standing the punch in a hot oven. Dickens was referring to the oven of a kitchen range, in which there was no naked light. In view of the spirit fumes, it is not safe to stand the hot mixture in either a gas or electric oven. The burning part of the process while quite effective visually was possibly necessary then to tone down the roughness or rawness of spirits before they became more refined.

No doubt Dickens was brewing this punch when he was at Doughty Street, and later, in *David Copperfield*, passed the mantle of expert punchmaker on to the shoulders of Mr Micawber. As he so aptly used to remark: 'But punch, my dear Copperfield, like time and tide, waits for no man.'[69] Standing in that dining-room, one can imagine the merry voices of the guests sitting around the table and almost savour the fragrant odours rising from that steaming bowl of delectable liquor.

CHAPTER 6

'The Great Unpaid'

'ANNUAL income twenty pounds, annual expenditure nineteen nineteen six, result happiness. Annual income twenty pounds, annual expenditure twenty pounds ought and six, result misery.'

Those were the words of advice given by John Dickens to his son Charles, and used by the novelist many years later for the character of Mr Micawber, in *David Copperfield*, based on his father. If only John Dickens had followed that advice, how much easier life would have been for his son!

In spite of his shortcomings, he was quite an extraordinary character, nearly as colourful as his fictional parallel, and it may be helpful to understand Dickens's attitude to him at Doughty Street by glancing at the background of John Dickens. In his burlesque extravaganza called *O'Thello*, Dickens rather appropriately cast his father for the part of The Great Unpaid.

The origins of John Dickens were certainly 'below stairs' and it is possible that from such beginnings came his rather grandiose outlook and actions and his desire to ape those above him and play the over-generous host. His father, William Dickens, was steward at Crewe Hall and his mother, Elizabeth Ball, a servant in Grosvenor Square. Later she was promoted to the post of housekeeper at Crewe. This is no doubt the source of Dickens's knowledge of life 'downstairs', which he put to such good use in many of his early sketches and later in *Dombey and Son*, in the downstairs household of the proud and pompous Dombey. The moods 'upstairs' are cleverly reflected in the moods 'downstairs' on such occasions as the wedding of Mr Dombey and the breaking up of his marriage:

All the servants have been breakfasting below. Champagne has grown too common among them to be mentioned, and roast fowls, raised pies, and lobster-salad have become mere drugs ... There is a general redness in the faces of the ladies ... Mr Towlinson has proposed the happy pair ... Mr Dombey's cook who generally takes the lead in society, has said it is impossible to settle down after this, and why not go, in a party, to the play?[1]

When Edith Dombey runs away and disgraces the proud family the mood downstairs alters accordingly:

Mr Dombey's servants are becoming, at the same time quite dissipated, and unfit for other service. They have hot supper every night and 'talk it over' with smoking drinks upon the board. Mr Towlinson is always maudlin after half past ten, and frequently begs to know, whether he didn't say that no good would ever come of living in a corner house! ... Cook ... entreats that you will never talk to her any more about people who hold their heads up, as if the ground wasn't good enough for them.[2]

Finally, when Mr Dombey becomes bankrupt and the staff are given notice by the housekeeper, and the cook is dismissed immediately:

Mr Towlinson's suggestion is, in effect, that Cook is going, and that if we are not true to ourselves, nobody will be true to us ... and that he thinks at the present time, the feelings ought to be 'Go one, go all!' The housemaid is much affected by this generous sentiment, and warmly seconds it ... It becomes a clear case that they must all go. Boxes are packed, cabs fetched, and at dusk that evening, there is not one member of the party left.[3]

In one of his early sketches, contributed to the *Evening Chronicle* in 1835, called 'The Four Sisters', Dickens is writing about the gossiping of the domestic staff at the street doors, the housemaid sweeping the steps at No. 23, etc.; also of domestic staff enjoying themselves at Greenwich Fair, and in 'London Recreations' he says:

The wish of persons in the humble classes of life, to ape the manners and customs of those whom fortune has placed above them, is often the subject of remark, and not unfrequently of complaint.

William Dickens, John Dickens's father, died in 1785, leaving his mother to bring up his brother and himself. Lord Crewe, Elizabeth's employer, made himself interested in the education of the two boys, and later obtained an appointment for John in the Navy Pay Office at Somerset

House, at £80 per annum. Here John Dickens met Thomas
Culliford Barrow, who had also been recently appointed
clerk in the same office. He and John became friends. John
Dickens eventually married his sister Elizabeth at St
Mary-le-Strand Church. Possibly John Dickens was residing
in the living accommodation at Somerset House at the time,
which would have entitled him to be married in the church in
that parish.

Elizabeth was a minor, so her father's consent to the
marriage had to be obtained. John Dickens, then twenty-
three, was so nervous that he started to sign his name in the
wrong place in the marriage register.[4] Was Dickens thinking
of this, one wonders, when in *Dombey and Son*, at the
marriage of Mr Dombey and Edith Granger, Cousin
Feenix, who gave the bride away, puts his name in the
wrong place, and enrols himself as having been born that
morning?[5]

Thomas Barrow's father and John Dickens's father-in-
law, Charles Barrow, had an important post in Somerset
House concerned with the payment of salaries in dockyard
towns, and was responsible for the purchase of furniture
and equipment. After an investigation it was discovered
that he had embezzled money to the extent of over £6000.
Naturally he was obliged to resign and criminal proceedings
were started against him. Before they could be put into
effect, he absconded to the Continent. Besides being a blow
to the family, this was certainly a blow to John Dickens,
as it seems quite likely that he had already been enjoying
some financial help from Charles Barrow with the rent of
a house in Portsmouth, since his marriage. Again and again
John applied to Thomas and John Barrow for money and
eventually, after many years, they refused to have anything
further to do with their brother-in-law. This is quite
apparent because at the time of his marriage Charles
Dickens wrote to his uncle, Thomas Barrow:

> There is no member of my family to whom I should be prouder to
> introduce my wife, than yourself, but I am compelled to say—and I am
> sure that you cannot blame me for doing so—that the same cause which
> has led me for a long time past, to deny myself the pleasure and advantage
> of your society, prevents my doing so. If I could not as a single man, I
> cannot as a married one, visit at a relation's house from which my father

is excluded: nor can I see any relatives here, who would not treat him, as they would myself.

After referring to the time when he visited Barrow in Gerrard Street during an illness—actually his uncle had broken a thigh—Dickens defends his father's character and says: 'Nothing that has occurred to me in my life, has given me greater pain, than thus denying myself the society of yourself and Aunt.'[6] This Gerrard Street house Dickens used later as the home of Mr Jaggers in *Great Expectations*.

No doubt Barrow was still smarting under the thought of the £200 he had stood guarantee for on behalf of John Dickens, and which he had been obliged to repay, not only the capital sum, but also six months' arrears of annuity, that John Dickens had contracted to pay and had failed to do so. Charles was only seven at that time when his father was 'cut off' by the Barrows. This was all reflected years later when, in *David Copperfield*, Mr and Mrs Micawber suffered the same fate with Mrs Micawber's family. (Mrs Micawber describes their reception as being 'decidedly cool'.)

In Portsmouth, John Dickens's extravagances were already landing him in difficulties, and when Charles was only a few months old, the family had to move into poorer premises, in Hawke Street. This property was destroyed in the great fire blitz on Portsmouth; it was very close to the docks, an obvious target. The birthplace, however, remains, refurnished as it possibly was when John and Elizabeth lived there with their baby Charles—a tribute to the memory of this famous son of Portsmouth.

After being summoned to London for a short time, during which the Dickens family lived in Norfolk Street, Fitzroy Square, John Dickens was appointed to Chatham and here, at 2 (now 11) Ordnance Terrace, his over-generous love of entertaining and making donations to local charities again brought the family finances low. During those days John Dickens lorded it among his friends and acquaintances proudly showing off the abilities of his children, particularly Charles, who was exhibited on a table in the local pub, the 'Mitre', singing such songs as 'The Cat's Meat Man', or duets with his sister, Fanny. Sometimes it would be walking up Gad's Hill, and grandly suggesting that hard work would take his small son into a house like the one he admired at the top of the hill. The house did of course become his home—Gad's Hill Place—many years after. This was one of his father's day dreams that really came true. Soon the pattern of Portsmouth was repeated: the family circumstances deteriorated and a smaller and a poorer house had to be found. They took one in 18 St Mary's Place, The Brook (now demolished). Even here they had two servants—Jane Bonny, whose name Dickens was to use in *Nicholas Nickleby*, spelt Bonney, and Mary Weller, whose name of course was immortalized in *Pickwick Papers*.

In 1822, John Dickens was transferred once more, this time to London. They lived in Camden Town, in a house in Bayham Street, later to become the humble home of Bob Cratchit in *A Christmas Carol*. Still the old financial troubles persisted: John Dickens got further and further into debt. One last desperate effort was made. Dickens's mother tried to run a school for girls and larger premises were taken at 4 Gower Street North at £50 per annum. A large plate was put on the front door, later taken away by the man who supplied it, because of course he had never been paid for it. The whole endeavour is humorously reproduced in *David Copperfield*, in which Mrs Micawber tries to retrieve the family fortunes by running a Young Ladies' Boarding Establishment. David, like young Charles, is sent round to distribute leaflets.

> I never found that any young lady had ever been to school there; or that any young lady ever came, or proposed to come; or that the least preparation was ever made to receive any young lady. The only visitors I ever saw or heard of, were creditors. They used to come at all hours and some of them were quite ferocious. One dirty-faced man, I think he was a boot-maker, used to edge himself into the passage as early as seven o'clock in the morning, and call up the stairs to Mr Micawber—'Come! You ain't out yet, you know. Pay us, will you? Don't hide, you know; that's mean. I wouldn't be mean if I was you. Pay us, will you? You just pay us, d'ye hear? Come!' Receiving no answer to these taunts, he would mount in his wrath to the words 'swindlers' and 'robbers'; and these being ineffectual too, would sometimes go to the extremity of crossing the street, and roaring up at the windows of the second floor, where he knew Mr Micawber was. At these times, Mr Micawber would be transported with grief and mortification, even to the length (as I was once made aware by a scream from his wife) of

making motions at himself with a razor; but within half-an-hour afterwards he would polish up his shoes with extraordinary pains, and go out, humming a tune with a greater air of gentility than ever. Mrs Micawber was quite as elastic. I have known her to be thrown into fainting fits by the king's taxes at three o'clock, and to eat lamb-chops breaded, and drink warm ale (paid for with two teaspoons that had gone to the pawnbroker's) at four. On one occasion when an execution had been put in, coming home through some chance as early as six o'clock, I saw her lying (of course with a twin) under the grate in a swoon, with her hair all torn about her face; but I never knew her more cheerful than she was, that very same night, over a veal cutlet before the kitchen fire, telling me stories about her papa and mama, and the company they used to keep.[7]

Much of the humour died, however, when Dickens turned the reality of the blacking factory into the fiction of the wine-bottling warehouse in *David Copperfield* : memories crowded in upon him of his father's arrest for the non-payment of a wine merchant's bill of £40, and his subsequent removal to the Marshalsea Debtors' Prison. When his mother joined his father in prison for economy, the eleven-year-old Dickens continued to lodge in the Camden Town district, with a Mrs Roylance. She, in *Dombey and Son*, became Mrs Pipchin, the ogress at Brighton. Later, his lodgings were moved nearer to the prison, to Lant Street, which was so splendidly used in *Pickwick* as the lodgings of the medical student, Bob Sawyer. His kindly and lame landlord and his wife became Mr and Mrs Garland in *The Old Curiosity Shop*.

In April 1824, John Dickens's mother died leaving him £450. She explained in her will that he already had had the rest of the money she would have left him. This enabled him to obtain his release, after three months in prison. During that time he had been retired from his employment on a disability pension of £145 per annum. His salary at the time of his retirement had reached £350 per annum. Charles was left in the blacking factory until, by chance, his father saw him exhibited in public, performing his work of labelling and wrapping the jars of shoe blacking. This was a blow to the pride of John Dickens, who hurriedly took Charles away and put him to school, in the Hampstead Road. His mother was in favour of patching up the quarrel and sending him back to the factory and this was un-doubtedly something he always resented and why, for the rest of their lives, Dickens seemed to be fonder of his father than of his mother.

During his Chatham days, John Dickens had occasionally shown a leaning towards journalism, and he now turned himself seriously to this calling, learning shorthand—any-thing but an easy task, and becoming a member of the Parliamentary Press—an avocation later to be taken up by his son.

For the next few years, as Dickens grew up, his father seems to have steered a more moderate course, and yet the many changes of address rather point to the urgent necessity of moving from time to time as arrears of rent piled up. From the time John Dickens obtained his release from the Debtors' Prison until his son moved independently into lodgings of his own so many addresses occur: a few of the better known ones were Little College Street, Johnson Street, The Polygon in Somer's Town, Fitzroy Street, Norfolk Street, Bentinck Street. Yet John Dickens seems to have kept himself just outside any serious trouble. It is a matter of wonder how long the legacy of £450 was made to last.

By the end of 1834, Charles had grown into manhood and John Dickens had again fallen into his old ways and reached yet another crisis in his life. The younger Dickens was working under considerable pressure to establish himself as a young journalist when suddenly, without warning, he awoke one morning to find that his father was again in trouble, arrested this time by the wine merchants Shaw and Maxwell.[8]

John Dickens had been taken to Abraham Sloman's detention house for debtors, in Cursitor Street, on his way once more to a debtors' prison. This sponging house was no doubt a model for the lock-up house of Mr Solomon Jacobs, so vividly described in 'Passage in the Life of Mr Watkins Tottle', contributed to *The Monthly Magazine* in 1835. Many details of the place may also have been used for Namby's Sponging House, Bell Yard, Cursitor Street, to which Mr Pickwick was conveyed before going into the Fleet Prison.[9]

Dickens himself may have been in danger of arrest, probably having backed his father's bills. In a postscript to his letter to Mitton he said that although he had not yet been taken no doubt that would be the next act in this 'domestic tragedy'.[10] He got together all the money he could from his friends, drew on his salary in advance, and as soon as he was free from work at six o'clock went to the sponging house. He managed to persuade the bill broker to renew the bill for two months, on paying the 'usual moderate bonus'. But his salary for a week or two was so completely mortgaged by the expenses of his own removal, that he was glad to avail himself of Beard's kind offer and borrow £5 for a short period.[11] He was even glad to borrow 'the enormous sum of 4/-' from Mitton, being 'rather hard up' that week.[12] And *Pickwick* was lurking just round the corner, his means of commanding hundreds of pounds— not shillings!

Even years later, Dickens was paying bills for his father. Writing to Forster in 1838, he mentioned that he had paid £57 2s. 6d. for Edward Barrow that morning. Directly he built up a hundred pounds, he wrote, one of his dear relations came along and knocked it down again.[13] Possibly Edward Barrow had signed a bill for John Dickens.

The moving expense he mentions followed the necessity of breaking up the home at Bentinck Street and finding separate accommodation. His two sisters, Fanny and Letitia, were fortunately just married and provided for. John Dickens was smuggled away to the home of Mrs Davis, the laundress, at North End, Hampstead, from whence he immediately applied to Beard for a loan of two sovereigns to replace his son Alfred's pumps, in which he was walking daily to Hampstead, and also the soles of his own shoes, which needed replacing. Mrs Dickens, with Alfred and Augustus, went into lodgings at 21 George Street, Adelphi, where she was later joined by her husband, still protesting that Beard should have his two sovereigns 'in a few days'. Dickens took his brother Frederick with him into chambers in Furnival's Inn.[14]

Comparative peace presumably reigned over the next year or so, during which time Dickens was married, moving first into larger quarters in Furnival's Inn and then into 48

Doughty Street. He was in some difficulty immediately after he moved for he had no dishes, no curtains, and no French polish. He therefore proposed that the projected house-warming should be postponed.[15] In yet another note he suggested going out to get dinner.[16]

His career began to take shape. To John Dickens, his son's astounding rise with its attendant financial advancement must have seemed a glittering and tempting outlook, and may quite conceivably have contributed to his own renewed extravagances.

By the end of 1837, Dickens had reluctantly undertaken the editing of *The Memoirs of Joseph Grimaldi*, the clown, for £300 and a half share of the profits. The manuscript was described by Bentley, who had bought it for £85, as 'somewhat illiterate'. Dickens's job entailed rewriting and re-arranging much of the material and John Dickens was employed by his son as amanuensis, work which he was no doubt very pleased to undertake. Life seems to have been fairly uneventful until the completion of this work and its publication, early in 1838. By the following year, John Dickens had once more managed to contract debts, unknown to his son. Directly he appreciated what the success of *Pickwick Papers* meant in financial language, John was approaching the publishers, Chapman and Hall, for £4 to 'tide him over'. In their kindness and generosity they felt they could not refuse such a small sum, but of course it soon grew into a larger figure, when John Dickens realized he had struck a gold mine. Before the first trifling sum had been repaid, he found himself in another difficulty. As in the case of Mr Micawber, John Dickens seemed to consider that the issue of a bill or promissory note was as good as paying off the debt.

It rather reminds me of the famous old music-hall sketch, 'A Sister to Assist 'Er', in which Fred Emney Senior, in the character of Mrs May, would negotiate a loan with his landlady. 'How much do you want?' asks the landlady. 'Twenty-five bob,' replies Mrs May. 'I've only got twenty-three,' says the landlady, counting out the money. 'All right,' replies Mrs May, promptly pocketing the money. 'You must howe me two!'

Before long, John Dickens was sending to Chapman and

Hall a promissory note for £20, from which he suggested they took the money outstanding, plus interest due, and send him the balance ! Failure to do so would 'be productive of fatal consequences'.[17] Here he rather slyly reminded them that their interests were bound up with those of his son. This ruse worked, maybe to John's surprise, but a month or so later he needed £15 to pay the rent, which unless paid by two o'clock, he was lost !

His total debt to Chapman and Hall soon reached £55, but he needed another £50 at once 'to save him from perdition'.[18] At this stage he offered to insure his life for £100 in favour of the publishers. He was soon apologizing to them for not paying his debt, owing to more pressing demands which threatened his liberty, having to be settled at once, and what is significant, thanking them for not telling his son. Yet, once again, he was arrested for debt and inviting the publishers to do what was necessary to get him out of his scrape.[19] In spite of selling scraps of manuscript and autographs to get money (and this possibly accounts for the scarcity of some of the earlier manuscripts of Dickens), he was again threatened with arrest by numerous tradesmen, of whom the wine merchant was undoubtedly to the fore.[20]

It was obvious that knowledge of his plight could not be withheld any longer from his son. One can imagine the feelings of Dickens when he was told of his father's involvement with his kindly and generous publishers. Quite obviously, something drastic had to be done quickly. Alfred, one of Dickens's brothers, had also been applying to Chapman and Hall for small loans.[21] His father and mother were left in doubt for no time at all that their brilliant son would brook no delay in putting them out of further temptation. There is a note from Dickens to his father, which though undated contains hints that it may belong to this period, which may well have been John's summons to Doughty Street to hear the Riot Act read: 'dine with us at half past five today'.[22] One can visualize the slightly penitent old prodigal (for he would never have entirely lost face) appearing a little humbly at No. 48, and no doubt trying to retain a vestige of his dignity. This was something to which Dickens never submitted Micawber, so maybe he also spared his father that ordeal, but he must have been far from pleased at the turn of events.

After carefully thinking things over, Dickens told Forster that he had booked on the Exeter coach for Monday, so that his parents could join him there when their notice expired on the following Saturday.[23] This notice refers to his parents' tenancy of 30 King Street, Holborn, yet another of their many temporary addresses. Dickens had undoubtedly been discussing his father's debts and shortcomings with Forster and had resolved to move them, with his youngest brother Augustus, then twelve years old, to Devonshire. His mother was to be with him the next morning and he had given her the choice of joining him at Exeter before his father as he thought she might get things in better order than he could (obviously, in the way of furnishing any premises Dickens found for them). The money for the coach-fares and road expenses was to be paid by Forster and Mitton to whom he was sending a cheque by post from Exeter.[24]

In London, 'The Great Unpaid' waited, wondering perhaps what was going to be done about him, maybe a little relieved that his son had taken responsibility once again for his difficulties. In spite of everything, he was rather a pathetic figure. How much he had been told or consulted is not clear, but he was certainly to be given no choice. It was not long before news came from Exeter.

CHAPTER 7

'A jewel of a place'

IN letters to Forster, his wife and Mitton, Dickens gave detailed accounts, sometimes quite amusing ones, of his adventures in Exeter and the successful culmination of his visit. It is best to relate them in his own words:

I cannot tell you what spirits I have been put into by the cottage I have taken—taken and paid the first quarter in advance!! I walked straight to it this morning. I heard nothing from the Bank and walked out to look about me. Something guided me to it, for I went on without turning right or left, and was no more surprised when I came upon it and saw the bill up, than if I had passed it every day for years. It is a jewel of a place—Mile End Cottage, Alpherton [*this should have been Alphington*]; the one mile stone from Exeter opposite the door. It is on the road to Plymouth, in the most beautiful, cheerful, delicious rural neighbourhood I was ever in. The old landlady, the finest old country-woman conceivable—lives next door, and her brother and his wife in the next cottage to that. They have been known there for half a century and have the highest possible character at the Bank and from the clergy-man who formerly lived himself, in the cottage which I have taken. I lunched with the old woman this morning, and we were quite affection-ate in no time. There is an excellent parlor with an open beaufet [buffet] in the wall and a capital closet, a beautiful little drawing room above that—a kitchen and a little room adjacent—and I forget whether two or three bedrooms besides. There is a noble garden, and there are cellars and safes and coalholes everywhere. The rent (including taxes) is £20 a year. The old lady has a 'lined' (she dwelt a good deal upon that) a 'lined' pew in the best part of the church, and in it are two sittings for nothing. The place is exquisitely clean and the paint and paper from top to bottom are as bright as a new pin. I have seen the upholsterer who furnished it when the clergyman lived there, and arranged with him for the greater part of the things. All articles here are cheap, even to furniture.

Then follow the instructions about his mother's proposed

85

journey on the Thursday, and the information that a cheque is enclosed to cover her fare and food on the way: 'She must eat and drink whenever and wherever the coach stops for the purpose. It goes from the Black Bear, Piccadilly, just beyond the Burlington Arcade.'[1]

To Forster he gives similar details and names the landlady:

Mrs Pannell of whom I must make most especial mention is a Devonshire widow with whom I had the honor of taking lunch to-day. She is a fat, infirm, splendidly fresh-faced country dame, rising sixty and recovering from an attack 'on the nerves' . . . In the event of my mother's being ill at any time, I really think the vicinity of this good dame (the very picture of respectability and good humour) will be the greatest possible comfort. *Her* furniture and domestic arrangements are a capital picture, but that with sundry imitations of herself and some 'ladies' who called while I was there (evidently with a view to the property) I must reserve 'till I see you, when I anticipate a hearty laugh. The cottages communicate at the back—that is, our people pass close behind hers to get to their garden.

The good lady's brother and his wife live in the next nearest cottage, and the brother transacts the good lady's business, the nerves not admitting of her transacting it herself, although they leave her in her debilitated state something sharper than the finest lancet. Now the brother having coughed all night till he coughed himself into such a perspiration that you might have wringed his hair, according to the asseverations of eye witnesses, his wife was sent for to negociate [sic] with me, and if you could have seen me sitting in the kitchen with the two old women, endeavouring to make them comprehend that I had no evil intentions or covert designs and that I had come down all that way to take some cottage and had *happened* to walk down that road and see that particular one, you would never have forgotten it. Then to see the servant girl run backwards and forwards to the sick man, and when the sick man had signed one agreement which I drew up and the old woman instantly put away in a disused tea-caddy, to see the trouble and number of messages it took before the sick man could be brought to sign another (a duplicate) that we might have one apiece, was one of the richest scraps of genuine drollery I ever saw in all my days. How, when the business was over, we became conversational—how I was facetious and at the same time virtuous and domestic—how I drank toasts in the beer, and stated on iterrogatary [sic] that I am a married man and the father of two blessed infants—how the ladies marvelled thereat—how one of the ladies, having been to London enquired where I lived and on being told, remembered that Doughty Street

and the Foundling Hospital were in the Old Kent Road, which I didn't
contradict,—all this and a great deal more must come ... when I
return, and will make us laugh then I hope, and makes me laugh now
to think of. Of my subsequent visit to the upholsterer's wife and the
timidity of the upholster[er], fearful of acting in her absence—of my
sitting behind a high desk in a little dark shop calling over the articles
in requisition and checking off the prices as the upholsterer exhibited
the goods and called them out—of my coming over the upholsterer's
daughter with many virtuous endearments to propitiate the establishment
and reduce the bill ...

He continues by mentioning that Charles Kean has been
at the local theatre, and when the theatrical company moved
on (it was presumably a one-night stand) he took over Kean's
sitting-room at the hotel in Exeter.[2]

Dickens wrote a second letter to his wife, as promised, in
which he gives her more details of the cottage and the
furniture he bought for it:

I have begun with the furniture which, with the exception of one or
two trifling articles, is contracted to be put in by Friday night. The
outside of every expense will be I hope Seventy Pounds. I trust it may
be done for less, but I take the very outside. I have put, or rather shall
put, into the worst sitting-room, six painted in imitation rosewood chairs,
a pembroke table, a round dining-table, a kidderminster carpet, and
some second-hand red curtains; cost price thirty shillings. In the best
sitting-room, six better chairs, a second-hand sofa table, a couch, white
muslin curtains, and a second-hand brussels carpet. In the best bedroom
a tent bedstead with best bedding and white dimity furniture; in the
next a french bed and mattress; and in both painted furniture en suite
of course. Then there are the kitchen necessaries, the crockery and
glass, the stair-carpet, and the floorcloth.[3]

To Thomas Mitton he repeats some of the details but
adds other interesting points:

I am on terms of the closest intimacy with Mrs Pannell the landlady,
and her brother and sister-in-law who have a little farm hard by. They
are capital specimens of country folks, and I really think the old woman
herself will be a great comfort to my mother. Coals are dear just now—
26/- a ton. They found me a boy to go two miles out and back again
to order some, this morning. I was debating in my mind whether I
should give him eighteen pence or two shillings when his fee was
announced—Twopence!
    The house is on the high road to Plymouth, and though in the very

heart of Devonshire, there is as much long-stage and posting life, as
you would find in Piccadilly. The situation is charming. Meadows in
front, an orchard running parallel to the garden hedge, richly-wooded
hills closing in the prospect behind, and away to the left, before, a
splendid view of the hill on which Exeter is situated; the Cathedral
towers rising up into the sky in the most picturesque manner possible ...
You would laugh if you could see me powdering away with the upholsterer, and endeavouring to bring all sorts of impracticable reductions
and wonderful arrangements. He had by him two second-hand carpets;
the important ceremony of trying the same, comes off at three this
afternoon ...[4]

Apparently Dickens was also making himself responsible
for the rent for his parents' old lodgings in King Street,
Holborn, which, as usual, was outstanding. He thought
it was £18, but he asked Mitton to see if his father could
get it reduced. Trying to spare his father's feelings, Dickens
asked Mitton to make believe when approaching John
Dickens that he did not know the reason for the move.

The two semi-detached cottages still stand on the Exeter/
Plymouth road, though now when walking from Exeter it is
necessary to go under the railway which has been constructed
since. The mile-stone from Exeter is, as far as I can
remember from when I was there about eighteen years ago,
somewhere near the railway arch and not opposite Mile End
Cottage as Dickens states. Various changes had taken place
before the time of my visit: the thatched roof had been
replaced by one of slate, and in the widening of the road,
the little front garden and wall had disappeared. Now, the
buses lumber past almost grazing the front of the house,
and people on top of the double-deckers can stare straight
into the upstairs bedrooms. Nor can the Cathedral towers
be seen, for houses have been built between the cottage and
Exeter, and now they can only be glimpsed occasionally
between the buildings when walking along the road. The
fate of the little cottage must have been in the balance over
the years. One more widening of the road on that side, and it
would disappear, leaving only a memory of John Dickens's
'suffering', his banishment to the country, an environment
to which he perhaps did not really belong. 'What can I do
in a little place like Alphington?' he rather pathetically
complained to Chapman and Hall. What indeed? Except

perhaps run up more bills! The publishers must have heaved a sigh of relief when he left London, as it must have been difficult for them to oblige him and at the same time be loyal to Dickens.

Dickens, somewhat optimistically, considered that he had put his parents out of harm's way; though, knowing his father, he must surely have entertained doubts still. He told Beard vaguely that he had made arrangements to settle his 'governor' for life.[5] His father was fifty-three at the time—a rather early age for complete retirement and rustication.

All this at a time when Dickens, still smarting from his encounters with publishers, was striving hard to make his mark in the world of literature, and cement the fame he had gained with the writing of *Pickwick Papers*. Financially he could just about cope with these setbacks, but his father could so easily have damaged his son's good name and standing when it was so important that he maintain a clean image before the public. Associations with bailiffs, sponging houses and debtors' prisons would hardly have done him much good. No doubt the exercise cost him quite a bit, perhaps more than he bargained for at first. In March we find him apologizing to his doctor for being unable to settle his bill, and offering £10 at the end of the month.[6] In a postscript to Mitton he writes: 'The King Street business has *almost* floored me.'[7] King Street had been his parents' lodgings and this admission points to the fact that no compromise had been possible over the matter of the outstanding rent; it may also indicate that further debts of his father's had come to light which had to be settled.

Soon he was receiving grumbling complaints through the post, and a month or so after settling John and Elizabeth in Devonshire, Dickens wrote to Forster: '... an unsatisfactory epistle from mother this morning.'[8] Again in July, he wrote: 'Read my mother's letter enclosed ... I do swear I am sick at heart with both her and father too, and think this *is* too much.'[9] It looks as if his mother did most of the complaining; at any rate, she appears to have been the spokeswoman. Maybe John held his son in too much awe to have much to say at that particular time.

By the end of July they seem to have settled down and, after a visit to Alphington, Dickens wrote to Forster:

I don't believe there is anywhere such a perfect little doll's house as
this. It is in the best possible order—beautifully kept—the garden
flourishing, the road lively, the rooms free from creeping things or any
such annoyance, and the prospect beautiful. I wish you could see it.[10]

One can imagine the novelty of this country life—such a
great contrast to the shabby lodgings the elder Dickenses
had been in and out of so frequently in London. Now, John
Dickens could strut about the village, a veritable squire in
his own domain; sailing into the private 'lined' pew on
Sundays, and doubtless boasting in the local public house
of his now quite famous son. However, where money was
concerned he was quite incurable. By 1841 he must have
contracted more debts, for on Dickens's instructions Mitton
put a somewhat vague notice in the Press, to the effect that
'certain persons having or purporting to have the surname
of our said client have put into circulation, with a view of
more readily obtaining credit thereon, certain acceptances
made payable at his private residence or at the offices of his
business agents. For the future no debts, other than those of
his own or his wife's contracting, would be paid.'[11] As he
pointed out to Mitton, he was more fearful than he could
tell of encouraging his father's expectations.[12] It was quite
apparent that John Dickens had been up to his old tricks in
drawing on bills in the name of Dickens, which creditors
would readily assume would be met by the son if not the
father. Even later in the year, such entries as 'Alphington,
£13' were appearing in Dickens's bank book, so he was still
having to find money for his father's debts.

On Dickens's return from America he again received
complaints from his parents about being shut away in
Alphington. Even as late as April 1844, Dickens told Mitton
that he was pressingly in need of £100 until June. His
father's debts, two quarters' income tax, etc. coming all at
once had driven him into a most uncomfortable corner.[13]
Through all this, it is significant that there seems to be no
record of any complaint from Kate that Dickens was spending so much money on his parents, much as she would have
had justification for making one.

John Dickens, though banished from London in the
Doughty Street days, was far from finished. In 1842,
Dickens agreed that he should be allowed back into London,

and four years later showed great faith in his ability by putting him in charge of the reporting staff of *The Daily News*, the newspaper Dickens had founded. He filled this post quite successfully. As Traddles said of Micawber, after the unmasking of Uriah Heep:

'Although he would appear not to have worked to any good account for himself, he is a most untiring man when he works for other people.'[14]

If Dickens's mother inspired any part of Mrs Micawber (her effort to help the family by endeavouring to start a school for young ladies was certainly a clear parallel), he seemed to deal very kindly with her through this character and her loyalty to her husband. Elizabeth was certainly loyal to John. With his father Dickens took a more tolerant view, looking upon him with the indulgence of a parent for a recalcitrant boy. 'I am vexed to hear that that father of mine . . . again. How long he is, growing up . . .'[15] (This letter, written by Dickens when he was in America, is torn and several words are missing, but its purport is clear.)

Some years later, John Dickens was to suffer a dreadful end, undergoing what was said to be the most terrible bladder operation in surgery—and without chloroform—from which he never recovered. He remained cheerful and strong-hearted to the end, according to Dickens.[16] He was to live again in the character of William Dorrit, but will always be remembered as the original of the immortal Wilkins Micawber, waiting confidently for something to turn up.

Whatever his shortcomings were, we shall for all time owe an everlasting debt to John Dickens, 'The Great Unpaid', for unwittingly giving the world Charles Dickens and Mr Micawber.

CHAPTER 8

'Bless his old gaiters'

'BLESS his old gaiters. He's a-keepin' guard in the lane with that 'ere dark lantern, like a amiable Guy Fawkes! I never see such a fine creetur in my days. Blessed if I don't think his heart must ha' been born five-and-twenty year arter his body at least!'[1]

So said Sam Weller in reference to his master, when Mr Winkle was having a secret meeting with Arabella one night at Clifton. Sam had become very fond of his master, and so had the readers of *Pickwick Papers* by that time.

Sam Weller is often looked upon as the saviour of *Pickwick Papers*. From being almost a failure at the beginning when only 400 copies were printed, the appearance of Sam Weller in the fourth number took the fancy of the readers, and before very long the sales rose to 40,000 a month.

It was early in 1836 that Dickens wrote to Chapman and Hall and made what he did not realize at the time was a very stupendous announcement: 'Pickwick is at length begun in all his might and glory. The first chapter will be ready tomorrow.'[2]

Three-fifths of *Pickwick Papers* had been written before Dickens moved to Doughty Street, so that by this time his name as author of that extraordinary first book was already well established. The other two-fifths, Chapters 34 to 57, had still to be written, however, and they constitute perhaps the most important part of the book. In that part, Mr Pickwick changed from an amusing old buffoon into somebody more human and serious, and the young author from being just a journalist—an exceptionally talented 'hack' writer who could make people laugh—into a serious contender for a place in the literary world, a writer with a message. During the change in Mr Pickwick's character, his young creator was gradually learning the art of literature and that is one of the very important things that happened at Doughty Street.

Part Thirteen, containing Chapters 34 to 36, was published after the move, but most of it had no doubt been written just before. Chapter 34 contained the account of the *Bardell v. Pickwick* case, in which Dickens used brilliantly his journalistic experience of reporting cases in court, in particular the *Melbourne v. Norton* case, which he had covered a short time before.

One of the first characters making his initial appearance in this part of the book is the amusing little judge, Mr Justice Stareleigh. It is generally accepted that he was based on Sir Stephen Gazalee (according to Edwin Pugh's book *The Dickens Originals*), whose name alone indicates a connection. Dickens's very amusing description was said also to have been applicable to the original:

> ... a most particularly short man, and so fat that he seemed all face and waistcoat. He rolled in upon two little turned legs, and having bobbed gravely to the bar, who bobbed gravely to him, put his little legs underneath his table and his little three-cornered hat upon it; and when Mr Justice Stareleigh had done this, all you could see of him was two queer little eyes, one broad pink face, and somewhere about half of a big and very comical looking wig.[3]

Serjeant Buzfuz also made his first appearance, as counsel for the plaintiff, Mrs Bardell, and was supposed to have been based on the real-life Serjeant Bompas. It is interesting also that R. S. Surtees, in his *Jorrock's Jaunts and Jollities*, lighted upon a similar name in a court case—Serjeant Bumptious.

This number of *Pickwick* contained the Pickwickians' visit to Bath, and the adventure of Mr Winkle in the Royal Crescent in his night attire. The following number included the delightful 'swarry' (soirée) at Bath, a most colourful event, with Sam Weller among the resplendent red, orange, yellow and blue uniforms of the Bath footmen. They all made their initial and brief appearance in the story with the unfortunate greengrocer, Harris, who provided the meal and was dubbed for his pains 'a wulgar beast'. Winkle at Bristol with Bob Sawyer and Benjamin Allen, and Sam Weller's search for Arabella, culminating in the episode involving Mr Pickwick, a dark lantern, and a credulous scientific gentleman—these were the ingredients for the light-hearted horseplay with which *Pickwick* abounds.

After the sudden and great blow of Mary Hogarth's death, the fount of humour was for a while stemmed. There was no instalment published the following month in June and we find Dickens consulting Forster about the wording of his notice explaining the break in the serial.[4] This was after his return from Hampstead, where he had been recovering from his shock.

The next day the young writer was back in harness again: 'I am getting on thank Heaven "like a house afire"—and think the next Pickwick will bang all the others. If you know anybody at Saint Paul's I wish you'd send round and ask them not to ring the Bell so.'[5] This was no doubt the bell that tolled early in the morning of 20 June on the death of William IV.

The number that was 'to bang all the others' was that which included the removal of Mr Pickwick into the Fleet Prison, and for the next two numbers a more serious note seems to have been struck—a protest against the custom of imprisonment for debt, without any limit on the length of the sentence and in such dreadful conditions. What comedy there is is somewhat grim until the end of Part Sixteen when Tony Weller brings his wife and the Rev. Stiggins to visit Sam in prison. Even then the serious note recurs and, after looking round the prison and witnessing the terrible squalor and suffering within those walls, Mr Pickwick throws himself into a chair in his little apartment and says, 'I have seen enough. My head aches with these scenes, and my heart too. Henceforth I shall be a prisoner in my own room.'[6] Lucky he was to have his own room, thanks to the Chancery prisoner from whom Mr Pickwick rented it.

Forster's review of this number of *Pickwick*, in *The Examiner*, spoke most highly of it, referring to the Fleet Prison chapters as his masterpiece and comparing them favourably with the writings of the greatest masters of this style of fiction.[7]

The Quarterly Review was not so kind to Dickens and was more critical of the later numbers of *Pickwick*. The reviewer expressed the opinion that Dickens wrote too

often and too fast and if he persisted in this course, after
rising like a rocket he would come down like a stick.[8]
Not a very sound prediction as it turned out, but no doubt
his astonishing success and popularity attracted a fair
amount of jealousy.

On the other hand, from America came not only praise,
but a desire to render to Dickens something of what was due
to him in spite of there being no international copyright.
There came from Philadelphia, not only an appreciation of
his work, but an offer to pay £25 or even £50 for twelve
parts of *Pickwick* already published by Carey, Lea and
Blanchard, booksellers and publishers from that city.
Dickens replied that it afforded him great pleasure to hear
about the popularity of *Pickwick* in America. He did not
feel justified in drawing upon them to the extent they
suggested, but would be quite happy to receive a copy of the
American edition of the book.[9] Later, when Dickens saw an
American edition of *Pickwick*, he complained to Leigh Hunt
of the singular vileness of the illustrations.[10]

One of the fairly rare mistakes that got by temporarily
in the proof correcting is referred to when Dickens wrote
direct to the printers, Bradbury and Evans:

> In the slip of Pickwick paged 675 at the 62nd line from the top I think
> I left uncorrected 'Master Raddle' for 'Master Bardell'. Will you have
> the goodness to see to this, and by substituting Master Bardell's name,
> to do justice to the memory of that distinguished child.[11]

In July, Dickens was busy on the sixteenth part, con-
taining Chapters 43 to 45. He sent an amusing letter to
Charles Hicks, marked 'Private and Confidential'. (Mr
Hicks was foreman printer to Bradbury and Evans.)

> To Mr Hicks.
> Oh, Mr Hick
> —S I'm heartily sick
> Of this sixteenth Pickwick
> Which is just in the nick
> For the publishing trick,
> And will read nice and slick,
> If you'll only be quick.
> I don't write on tick,
> That's my comfort, Avick![12]

On the question of using fact in his fiction, Dickens wrote that month to Mr George Beadnell, the banker, whose daughter Maria Dickens had unsuccessfully courted some seven years previously. George Beadnell had apparently sent Dickens a story by a Mr Clarke for inclusion in *Pickwick Papers*:

> ... if I were in the slightest instance whatever, to adopt any information so communicated, however much I invented upon it, the World would be informed one of these days—after my death perhaps—that I was not the sole author of The Pickwick Papers ... that a gentleman in the Fleet Prison perfectly well remembered stating in nearly the same words—&c &c &c. In short I prefer drawing upon my own imagination in such cases. Mr Clarke's own story I have put into a Cobbler's mouth who tells it in the next number; and this is the only reality in the whole business of and concerning the Fleet. Fictitious narratives place the enormities of the system in a much stronger point of view, and they enable one to escape the personalities and endless absurdities into which there is a certainty of rushing if you take any man's account of his own grievances.[13]

In other words, fiction is stronger than fact.

Thus, in *Pickwick*, Sam Weller questions the cobbler, his fellow prisoner with whom he shares a room, about the reasons for his being in the Fleet Prison:

> 'Ah,' said the cobbler, 'you don't quite understand this matter. What do you suppose ruined me now?' 'Why,' said Sam, trimming the rushlight, 'I s'pose the beginnin' wos that you got into debt, eh?' 'Never owed a farden,' said the cobbler; 'try again.' 'Well, perhaps,' said Sam, 'you bought houses, wich is delicate English for goin' mad, or took to buildin', wich is a medical term for bein' incurable.' 'The fact is I was ruined by having money left me.'[14]

The cobbler explains that a legacy of £5000 had been left by someone he worked for and whose relative he had married. One thousand was to be for himself and the rest to be divided among various nieces and nephews. Although he distributed the money to them, they took him to court because they did not get all the £5000.

> 'The case comes on some months afterwards,' continued the cobbler, 'afore a deaf old gentleman in a back room somewhere down by Paul's Churchyard; and arter four counsels had taken a day apiece to bother him regularly, he takes a week or two to consider, and read the evidence

Charles Dickens in 1837,
by S. Laurence

Mrs Charles Dickens,
by D. Maclise

Harley in
The Strange Gentleman

John Hullah

St James's Theatre

Covent Garden Theatre

W. C. Macready

Grimaldi

Mary Hogarth's grave

Mary Hogarth, by Maclise

Collins's Farm, 1832

'Phiz' (H. K. Browne),
by himself

Shaw's Academy (original of Dotheboys Hall)

John Forster   Thomas Beard

Harrison Ainsworth

Robert Cruikshank,
sketched by himself

C. Dickens,
by Cruikshank

Daniel Maclise

John Dickens

Mrs Elizabeth Dickens

Mile End Cottage, Alphington

The parlour, Mile End Cottage

The drawing-room, Mile End Cottage

Charley, Mary, Katie and Baby Wally, by Maclise

Elm Cottage, Petersham

Jack Straw's Castle, Hampstead

The 'Star and Garter', Richmond

12 High Street, Broadstairs

Albion Hotel, Broadstairs

Fort House, Broadstairs

Works
written at
Doughty Street

Mr Pickwick slides

Oliver asking for more

*The Yorkshire
Schoolmaster at the
Saracen's Head
(Nicholas Nickleby)*

Playbill:
The Village Coquettes, etc.

48 Doughty Street

1 Devonshire Terrace

Mr. Pickwick leaving Doughty Street

in six vollums, and then gives his judgment that how the testator was not quite right in his head, and I must pay all the money back again and all the costs. I appealed; the case come on before three or four very sleepy gentlemen, who had heard it all before in the other court, where they're lawyers without work; the only difference being that there they're called doctors, and in the other place delegates, if you understand that; and they very dutifully confirmed the decision of the old gentleman below. After that we went into Chancery, where we are still, and where I shall always be. My lawyers have had all my thousand pound long ago; and what between the estate, as they call it and the costs, I'm here for ten thousand, and shall stop here till I die, mending shoes . . .'[15]

The Chancery prisoner does die and so gets his discharge. Dickens was of course drawing partly on his recollection and experience of the courts in Doctors' Commons and partly anticipating the Chancery case in *Bleak House*, and the man from Shropshire, Gridley.

Dickens knew the interior of a debtors' prison only too well from the days when he visited his father in the Marshalsea; and also about sponging houses, having several times rescued his father from those dreadful places. He could therefore quite easily people the Fleet Prison scenes with appropriate characters—the turnkey, Tom Roker, the disreputable inmates such as Mivins, Smangle, Martin, and so on. It seems likely however, that he must have acquired some knowledge of the geography of the Fleet, because he describes it all in such detail—the racket ground, the 'Painted Ground', with its pictures of men-of-war in full sail on the walls, the whistling shop, the Coffee-Room Flight, and the rest. It is possible that he might have arranged a visit to the prison in the guise of a reporter, as he had for Newgate Prison, but if he did, it seems strange that there appears to be no correspondence on the matter, as in the case of Newgate. It rested with Dickens to make people aware of these fearful places and the misery suffered inside them. That he did in no uncertain manner, first in *Pickwick* and later in other books, principally *Little Dorrit*.

He certainly availed himself of the opportunity of pointing to the unfair treatment meted out to debtors compared with that afforded to those guilty of criminal offences, which included the inmates of Newgate. Whereas criminals in Newgate were fed—perhaps for a limited time only, many of them being bound for the gallows—those in debtors' prisons, unless they could pay for it, were barely fed at all. The poor debtors without any money had to pawn the very clothes they stood up in, or take it in turns to beg for alms at a grille looking on to the street. When Mr Pickwick meets Mr Jingle in the Fleet, the following conversation takes place:

'You have forgotten your coat.'

'Eh?' said Jingle. 'Spout—dear relation—Uncle Tom—couldn't help it—must eat you know. Wants of nature and all that.'

'What do you mean?'

'Gone, my dear sir—last coat—can't help it. Lived on a pair of boots—whole fortnight. Silk umbrella—ivory handle—week—fact——honour—ask Job—knows it.'

'Lived for three weeks upon a pair of boots and a silk umbrella with an ivory handle!' exclaimed Mr Pickwick, who had only heard of such things in shipwrecks . . .[16]

'Take that, sir,' said Mr Pickwick to Job Trotter. Take what? Not a blow as it might have been, but something from Mr Pickwick's waistcoat pocket that chinked.[17] So Mr Pickwick, now a real person of flesh and blood and human feelings, is given an opportunity of displaying clemency to an old enemy who has hitherto hoodwinked him and treated him shabbily.

Among the letters on display at the Dickens House Museum is an amusing—and somewhat revealing—one to Chapman and Hall, in which Dickens says: 'When you have quite done counting the sovereigns, received for Pickwick, I should be most obliged to you, to send me up a few.'[18] He should have received this payment on 1 August 1836, and he was obviously relying upon receipt of the money, as he was not so well off at that time.

Forster at one time called Dickens's attention to one of the several piracies of *Pickwick Papers*, written by the dramatist W. T. Moncrieff and entitled *Sam Weller; or the Pickwickians*. It was really a dramatic adaptation and Forster had incurred the wrath of its author by writing an unfavourable criticism of the production when it was presented at the Strand Theatre. Dickens's reaction was:

. . . if the *Pickwick* had been the means of putting a few shillings in the vermin-eaten pockets of so miserable a creature, and has saved him from a workhouse or a jail, let him empty out his little pot of filth and welcome. I am quite content to have been the means of relieving him.[19]

Forster had been abused by Moncrieff in the preface to the adaptation and one wonders whether Dickens's passive attitude to the piracy really satisfied his friend.

Several celebration dinners were held during the writing of *Pickwick* and on its completion. Chapman and Hall gave the first one to mark the first anniversary, on which occasion they presented the young author, then only twenty-five, with an honorarium of £500, over and above the payment already agreed. Dickens himself gave a dinner at Dejex's, 1 Leicester Place, Leicester Square, originally planned for October, to mark the conclusion of the writing of the book, but it was postponed until November, 1837. A number of his friends and business acquaintances were invited— Ainsworth, Hill, Hicks, Macready, Lover, Browne, Forster, Talfourd, Cruikshank and John Dickens were among those who attended, and the evening cost Dickens £41 7s., according to his bank book (on view at Dickens House).

In the same month Chapman and Hall gave yet another banquet at the Prince of Wales Tavern, Leicester Square, to celebrate the completion of the work. 'The head waiter . . . entered and placed a glittering temple of confectionery on the table, beneath the canopy of which stood a little figure of the illustrious Pickwick.'[20] Once again the publishers made a present to Dickens over and above the normal payment, this time of £750. With £500 of this Dickens opened an account with Coutts Bank, and began at last to enjoy some substance for his efforts and put something by for contingencies—no longer living from hand to mouth as it were. Chapman and Hall also presented him with a set of silver apostle spoons, with Pickwickian characters on the handles, the whereabouts of which are not now known.

A great wave of Pickwickian popularity set in and numerous souvenirs appeared, just as in more recent years the Disney figures have invaded the shops. There were innumerable china and metal figurines and a great number of articles named after Pickwick and Sam Weller—pens, cigars, canes, etc., songs, duets and other musical novelties. People named their pets after the characters, too. Dickens himself did that years later, though not from Pickwick;

he had a dog called Bumble and horses named Trotty Veck and Newman Noggs. Even as this book is being written more solid silver figurines of the Pickwickian characters are being modelled.

When Dickens came to Doughty Street, much important work on *Pickwick* had still to be done. Out of a total of 250 characters in the complete book, more than seventy had still to be introduced for the first time, and many pages still to be written. Moving beyond the work's light-hearted humour, he seized the opportunity for more serious writing —a satire on the legal system in *Bardell v. Pickwick* and a tilt against the debtors' prisons, their appalling conditions and the system that could shut people up for life, in the Fleet chapters; but with this endeavour to write to some purpose, the primary aim to entertain and to attain popularity was not forgotten, for this ensured that there would be bread and butter for his dependents.

Nor could he resist a tilt at the newspapers, having so recently worked in journalism, and to point to their astonishing abuse of their competitors. The leading articles of the two rival papers, *The Eatanswill Gazette* run by Mr Pott and *The Eatanswill Independent* run by Mr Slurk, were in no way an exaggeration of London newspapers of the day.

When Dickens as a young journalist managed to beat *The Times* back to London with news of Lord John Russell's election campaign in Devonshire, that sedate newspaper referred to *The Morning Chronicle* as 'that squirt of filthy water' and a 'licentious feeder on falsehood and lies'. *The Morning Chronicle* retorted with 'the poor old *Times*, in its imbecile ravings, resembles those unfortunate wretches whose degraded prostitution is fast approaching neglect and disgust'. *The Standard* called *The Globe* 'our blubber-headed contemporary' and *The Morning Chronicle* referred to *The Morning Post* as 'that slop-pail of corruption'.[21]

Writing of the death of Mrs Weller, Dickens perhaps attained a peak of genuine pathos—pathos that can still be appreciated today, because it is so skilfully mixed with that touch of humour; in other words, life has not changed— it is still a mixture of laughter and tears in very close proximity. This passage we can still accept, while the constant playing on readers' emotions in the descriptions of the deaths of Little Nell and Paul Dombey is no longer palatable for the present-day reader. The appeal of such pitiful scenes has disappeared with the conception of angelic harp playing and of fiery consumption in eternal Hell.

Consoling his father on the death of Mrs Weller, Sam says:

'Vell, gov'nor, ve must all come to it one day or another.'

'So we must, Sammy,' said Mr Weller the elder.

'There's a Providence in it all,' said Sam.

'O' course there is,' replied his father with a nod of grave approval. 'Wot 'ud become of the undertakers vithout it, Sammy?'[22]

Tony Weller was no doubt typical of many old coachmen who plied their trade on the road when Dickens was using this means of travel during his journalistic career. As a reporter he used the coaches owned and run by Moses Pickwick, and it was seeing that name on the side of the coach that gave him the name of that immortal character. Moses Pickwick had his headquarters at Bath and from here he ran services to London and to the West—Devonshire and Cornwall. Whilst occupied in writing this book I was shown by a solicitor friend of mine the records of a court case brought against Moses Pickwick by a passenger named Brooke, on 26 May 1827—the year of *Pickwick*. It was an action brought against the coach proprietor in order to recover damages for the loss of a trunk from a coach travelling from Bath to Truro. The verdict went against Moses Pickwick and an application for re-trial on the grounds of mis-direction was dismissed. It is interesting to note that one Justice Gaselee commented upon this application and agreed with the decision. One wonders if he was the Justice Gazalee who is said to be (by Edwin Pugh in *The Dickens Originals*) the original of Justice Stareleigh in the *Bardell v. Pickwick* case.[23]

Dickens made gifts of several presentation copies of *Pickwick Papers*, including one to Serjeant Talfourd, to whom Dickens dedicated the book, in recognition of his attempts to get his Copyright Bill through Parliament. The author also received 'extra super bound' copies of *Pickwick* from the publishers, one of which he sent to Forster,[24] one to Harrison Ainsworth[25] and one he gave to his wife Kate. He also sent a special copy bound in blue levant morocco with gilt edges by Rivière, to Mrs Henry Belcombe, wife of H. S. Belcombe, M.D., a frequent contributor to medical journals. It was accompanied by a note in which he said that the zeal of his publishers had put it into a much smarter dress than his own modesty might have suggested as an appropriate costume.[26] In his letter to Forster, Dickens referred to his son Charley: 'Our boy took the measles last Saturday to celebrate his birthday, and has been ill ever since. "He's got 'em very mild" in nursery phrase, so I am not sorry for it as it will now be quickly over.'

As he approached the completion of *Pickwick*, Dickens found it necessary to excuse himself from an engagement with Talfourd, as he had 'two Pickwicks' to write. He referred of course to the double number at the end, containing Parts Nineteen and Twenty, a custom he always followed afterwards.[27] In his criticism of *Pickwick Papers*, Professor Edgar Johnson wrote: 'Almost all the events in *Pickwick* are related in a sedate and even solemn manner that intensifies their humour.'[28] This is the real secret of the humour of *Pickwick*—the dignity of its chubby central character, a 'fairy in tights and gaiters' (as Sam Weller terms him) who is subjected to outrageous events. Lose the dignity of Mr Pickwick and you have lost a greater part of the comedy. That is where many would-be portrayers of the character have slipped up in the past.

In writing the concluding lines of this unique book Dickens could almost have said, with truth, the words of Mr Pickwick as he took his farewell: 'If I have done but little good, I trust I have done less harm.'

Even before Dickens came to Doughty Street, he was writing to his publishers:

> If I were to live one hundred years, and write three novels in each, I should never be so proud of any of them, as I am of Pickwick, feeling as I do, that it has made its own way, and hoping, as I must own I hope, that long after my hand is withered as the pens it held, Pickwick will be found on many a dusty shelf with many a better work.[29]

How right he was, but I query the provision 'with many a better work'. There can only be one Pickwick!

CHAPTER 9

'The parish boy's progress'

FROM November 1837, when the writing of *Pickwick Papers* was finished, until about February 1838, Dickens had only one book to consider, *Oliver Twist*, and was free from having to write two books at the same time. From February 1838, when he started his new novel, *Nicholas Nickleby*, for Chapman and Hall, until the completion of *Oliver Twist* and its publication in three volumes, he once again had two stories with which to contend.

His general plan seems to have been to write the *Oliver* instalment first each month before attempting one for *Nickleby*, but he did not fulfil the provisions of his agreement with Chapman and Hall to write and deliver the manuscript to the publishers by the 15th of each month.[1]

Imagine, for a moment, that you have a flair for writing, and in particular a flair for character creation, and that you are to write a story equivalent in quality to the opening of *Oliver Twist*. You would find it difficult. But imagine writing at the same time something equivalent to the last twenty-three chapters of *Pickwick Papers*, and during the last twenty-six chapters of *Oliver Twist*, the first chapters of a story of the calibre of *Nicholas Nickleby*: then you will begin to appreciate the ability and drive of Dickens and to have a real respect for what was nothing short of genius. That is what Dickens did, besides carrying on the editorship of a magazine (*Bentley's Miscellany*), the editorship of a biography (*The Memoirs of Grimaldi*), the supervision and publication of a special book for charity (*The Pic Nic Papers*, for Macrone's widow), sundry theatrical activities and a running dispute with two publishers, besides coping with a rather troublesome private life. That was the lot of Dickens between the ages of twenty-four and twenty-seven at Doughty Street.

Dickens has been pilloried by some critics for not using realistic language or situations for his characters of the street and the underworld—language and events he knew only too well from his life in the blacking factory days and his familiarity with life in debtors' prisons. But, I ask, would his powerful indictment of the treatment of helpless paupers have been strengthened one jot by introducing scenes with slop-pails and lavatories; or the impact of a prostitute's sordid sacrifice have been advanced one iota by a detailed account of Sikes stripping off her frowsy rags in a foul garret; or the power of a burglar's brutish character have been made more convincing by his repetitive use of four-letter words and oaths? Dickens very wisely left this to the imagination of his readers, and yet the atmosphere he aimed at is all there with a surety that no modern writer can command. He may in this respect have been a slave to the conventions of his time, but so are modern writers to theirs, and to the present cult of withholding nothing. In my opinion, they fail dismally by becoming all alike, as modern buildings have, and exceedingly boring!

The differences between *Pickwick Papers* and *Oliver Twist* are manifest: a much smaller canvas is used this time, with only fifty-seven characters, but one great difference is that *Pickwick Papers* was originally unplanned and *Oliver Twist* was planned. *Pickwick* was written practically from the word go, when William Hall of Chapman and Hall called on Dickens and asked him to supply the copy for a series of humorous sporting sketches by Robert Seymour, an established artist. Professor Tillotson, in the Clarendon edition of *Oliver Twist*, expresses the opinion that this story was planned as early as 1833. Dickens probably had in mind even then the writing of a novel; his sketches at that time were related to 'the Parish', and its officers and inhabitants and his thoughts were tending in the direction of the main subject of *Oliver Twist*, the sub-title of which is 'The Parish Boy's Progress'.

He told Bentley that he had hit on a capital notion, and one which would bring Cruikshank out.[2] This seems rather cheeky on the part of Dickens, suggesting that Cruikshank, a quite famous artist, would benefit from his choice of subject, but then Dickens had the last part of *Pickwick* behind him, and was beginning to realize that his own name and prestige really meant something. The result of this idea was the first illustration in the book, 'Oliver asks for more'. This took Oliver round the world, to practically every country, and to call oneself an 'Oliver Twist' came to indicate that one wanted some more.

The first instalment of *Oliver* appeared in *Bentley's Miscellany* in the February (1837) number of that magazine. The first issue of this number was attributed to 'Boz' on the title page, but soon Dickens asked Bentley to substitute his name in the advertisements in place of Boz. Later issues and editions were amended accordingly and the name of Boz disappeared.[3] As soon as he had written the instalment he was asking the publisher whether he had seen *Oliver Twist* yet, as he (Dickens) had taken a great fancy to Oliver, and hoped the boy deserved it.[4] The following month both he and his wife were ill, and after completing twelve and a half pages out of the prescribed sixteen, he told Bentley that he could not possibly write any more under these combined circumstances. But, he pointed out, he had thrown his whole heart and soul into *Oliver Twist*. Bentley in his prolonged dispute with Dickens, in respect of these pages short, in spite of additional material being supplied to supplement the shortages, was later to deduct so much from his payment to Dickens. This niggardly attitude on Bentley's part annoyed the author immensely (see Chapter 4).

The underworld characters in *Oliver Twist* represented a class which normally would not have appeared in stories intended for the family circle. Readers were aware of the existence of poor people, of course—vaguely aware of them, and for them, that was sufficient. So Dickens really set out to shock his readers—those comfortable families gathered round their blazing drawing-room fires—into becoming aware of young children in workhouses and similar institutions, dirty, inadequately fed and clothed, and also of the young boys, sometimes only five years old, who were made to climb those chimneys to sweep them clear of soot, and sometimes lost their sight and even their lives in doing so. In February, Dickens was advising Cruikshank that it would be better to leave illustrating Oliver's master and mistress (the Sowerberrys) until the next number. He had therefore interposed Gamfield, the sweep, and in doing so struck a powerful blow for the little boys cruelly made to climb chimneys.[5]

'It's a nasty trade,' said Mr Limbkins, when Gamfield had again stated his wish.

'Young boys have been smothered in chimneys before now,' said another gentleman.

'That's acause they damped the straw afore they lit it in the chimbley to make 'em come down agin,' said Gamfield; 'that's all smoke, and no blaze; vereas smoke ain't o' no use at all in making a boy come down, for it only sinds him to sleep, and that's wot he likes. Boys is wery obstinit, and wery lazy, gen'lmen, and there's nothink like a good hot blaze to make 'em come down vith a run. It's humane too, gen'lmen, acause even if they're stuck in the chimbley, roasting their feet makes 'em struggle to extricate theirselves.'[6]

Comedy, yes—but grim comedy, angry comedy, to get his point over to his readers. Comedy to shock them and make them shudder, but maybe to lend their support towards getting these dreadful customs changed. As the fat boy in *Pickwick* said to the old lady: 'I wants to make your flesh creep.'

Sir Francis Burdett, Tory M.P. for North Wilts, father of Angela Burdett Coutts, with whose work for charity Dickens was later to become so closely associated, wrote to tell his daughter that he had finished the first volume of *Oliver Twist*, and although interesting it was very painful, and disgusting, and as the Old Woman of Edinburgh remarked, on hearing a preacher describing the sufferings of Jesus Christ, he hoped it wasn't true. Whether anything like it existed or not, he meant to make an enquiry, for it was quite dreadful and to society in the country, very distasteful. He intended to finish it but found it anything but entertaining.[7]

For many people at that time, the attitude was one of grudging admission that maybe the poor and starving did exist, but they did not want to be told about it. As Podsnap in *Our Mutual Friend* dismissed unpleasant subjects with a wave of his hand, so would many of Dickens's contemporaries. Ainsworth also wrote about people of the lower classes—highwaymen, etc., but he glamorized them, and so they became acceptable—like MacHeath in Gay's

Beggar's Opera; but Dickens knew it was important to write forthrightly about felons and prisons and criminals, and more important still that people knew of their existence in the real world.

Dickens was anxious to maintain within reason some factual accuracy in criticizing the effects of the New Poor Law of 1834, and to this end consulted certain official statistics. He described the action of the Board of Guardians as establishing a rule

> that all poor people should have the alternative (for they would compel nobody, not they) of being starved by a gradual process in the house, or by a quick one out of it. With this view, they contracted with the water-works to lay on an unlimited supply of water; and with a corn-factor to supply periodically small quantities of oatmeal; and issued three meals of thin gruel a day, with an onion twice a week, and half a roll on Sundays.[8]

This was the diet for children and was purposely exaggerated for effect, but not to an unreasonable extent. The No. 1 Dietary approved and published by the Poor Law Commissioners in 1836 (and Dickens would no doubt have consulted this) included 1½ pints of gruel daily and the diet was varied during the week—adding to the gruel on three days, 12 ounces of bread, 5 ounces of cooked meat, ½ pound of potatoes and 1½ pints of broth; on three other days, 1½ pints of soup and 2 ounces of cheese were substituted for the broth; on Fridays, 14 ounces of suet or rice pudding with 12 ounces of bread, 1½ pints of gruel and 2 ounces of cheese. This was divided into three meals a day; women and children over nine got less and children under nine were to be fed 'at discretion'—a very ominous provision. The *Oliver Twist* diet therefore was not far away from the fact.[9]

After the publication of Part Four in May 1837, finishing at Chapter 8, where Oliver is installed in Fagin's den, came the sudden tragedy of Mary Hogarth's death. Nothing had been written for the next part and Dickens felt himself quite incapable of writing. The same interruption which applied to *Oliver* of course applied to *Pickwick* as well.

There was also another break in the appearance of the monthly instalment of *Oliver* in October of that year.

Dickens was having his dispute with Bentley at the time and threatened to stop writing the serial. Possibly he left it too late to write it, because he eventually substituted a long paper called *The Mudfog Association*.

In November, the following month, Dickens expressed pleasure that Forster liked that month's *Oliver* and especially that he praised the first chapter in particular. This was Chapter 16, in which Oliver, after being recaptured, is protected by Nancy, who turns on Fagin when the Jew threatens the boy. Dickens said that he hoped to do great things with Nancy, especially if he could work out the idea he had formed about the female with whom she was to be contrasted.[10] This was obviously Rose Maylie, but it was not until a year later that he introduced her into the story. Then, quite clearly basing her on Mary, he found that he had not the courage to kill her in all her youth and beauty and so she recovers, in the story, from her serious illness.

Dickens called Bentley's attention to a very favourable report of *Oliver Twist* in the *Edinburgh Review*, which said that it was better than anything Dickens had written before, 'admirably told', and possessing 'perfect truthfulness in the generality of his characters'.[11]

The humour and lighter side of the story was sustained chiefly by Bumble, although Dickens was using him to hold beadles up to scorn. His great friend Serjeant Talfourd on one occasion sent Dickens some sparkling Moselle. In thanking him, the author said that he would try its inspiration and that *Oliver* would be lighter that month. It certainly was lighter as the number contained the famous Bumble and Corney courtship.[12]

On resuming the story after Mary's death, Dickens continued by describing Oliver in Fagin's den in Field Lane. Field Lane led to Saffron Hill, in which district were shops where silk handkerchiefs could be bought from pickpockets. Field Lane has gone but Saffron Hill still remains. This part also contained the training of the boys to pick pockets and Oliver's involvement in the stealing of Mr Brownlow's handkerchief and his appearance in the police court. In his journalistic work Dickens had reported on the activities of the notorious magistrate Laing, in *The Morning Chronicle* of 24 November 1835,[13] and he decided to use him in the story. In this instance, there is no doubt about the identity of the original on whom the character was based. Wishing to see this magistrate in action, Dickens wrote to Haines, a reporter in the Mansion House police office, asking to be smuggled into the Hatton Garden Police Court where Laing operated.[14] The following description was the result:

> Mr Fang was a lean, long-backed, stiff-necked, middle-aged man, with no great quantity of hair, and what he had growing on the back and sides of his head. His face was stern and much flushed. If he was really not in the habit of drinking rather more than was exactly good for him, he might have brought an action against his countenance for libel, and have received heavy damages.[15]

A. S. Laing, the original of this remarkable portrait, continued to abuse his office and was eventually dismissed from the Bench. Dickens did not receive any protest from that original, but he did on another occasion regarding the callous conduct of the clergyman at the pauper's funeral attended by Oliver:

> Immediately afterwards the clergyman appeared putting on his surplice as he came along ... the reverend gentleman, having read as much of the burial service as could be compressed into four minutes, gave his surplice to the clerk and walked away again.[16]

Marcus Stone, one of Dickens's illustrators, in a speech at the Boz Club Dinner in 1910 mentioned his walks with Dickens from Gad's Hill. On one occasion they came to Cooling and Dickens pointed out the church where he actually saw a pauper's funeral taking place exactly as he described it. A few months after the description was published Dickens received a letter from a clergyman asking whether it were possible that such a thing could occur. He was in fact the clergyman at the church pointed out to Marcus Stone, and Dickens replied to his letter: 'Thou art the man.'[17]

Sir Peter Laurie, alderman of London, told a public meeting in 1850 that Jacob's Island existed only in a work of fiction written by Mr Charles Dickens ten years ago. In his preface to the 'Cheap Edition of *Oliver Twist*' in 1850, Dickens replied that reflecting upon this logic ... when Fielding described Newgate, the prison immediately ceased to exist; that when Smollett took Roderick Random to Bath, that city instantly sank into the earth; that when Scott exercised his genius on Whitefriars, it incontinently glided into the Thames; that an ancient place called Windsor was entirely destroyed in the reign of Queen Elizabeth by two Merry Wives of that town, acting under the direction of a person of the name of Shakespeare; and that Mr Pope, after having at a great expense completed his grotto at Twickenham, incautiously reduced it to ashes by writing a poem upon it. Sir Peter Laurie having been himself described in a book . . . it is but too clear that there CAN be no such man !

A Mrs Eliza Davis also protested to Dickens that he was unfair to the Jewish race in making such a terrible villain as Fagin a Jew. She also asked him for a donation for the benefit of the Jewish poor. In sending his donation, he replied: 'Fagin, in Oliver Twist, is a Jew, because it unfortunately was true of the time to which that story refers that that class of criminal almost invariably was a Jew, but all the rest of the wicked dramatis personae are Christians.'[18] Later, in *Our Mutual Friend*, Dickens created a Jewish character, Riah, who is so exceptionally good that he is almost too good to be true. Mrs Davis presented Dickens with a copy of *Benisch's Hebrew and English Bible*.

I always remember an occasion during one of my lecture recitals, when I thought a member of the audience was staging a protest against Fagin. It was in the Cripplegate or Golden Lane Theatre as it is now known, in the City of London, and I was giving the excerpt where Fagin was gloating over his treasures and finds Oliver watching him. A lady in the front row got up, walked up the centre aisle and out of a door at the back. In a few moments, however, she came in again by a side door and sat down. At the end of the evening during the questions and discussion, I found that just before the lecture began this lady had been washing her hands in the cloakroom. When I mentioned Fagin taking out of his box a gold watch followed by at least half a dozen more, some rings, brooches and bracelets, the lady remembered she had left her ring on the wash basin, and had returned to fetch it. A unique moment in the career of Fagin—restoring someone's lost ring !

The name Fagin undoubtedly came from that of Bob Fagin, a rough boy who was kind to Dickens when as a boy he worked in the blacking warehouse. He looked after Dickens when he was taken ill on more than one occasion and once took him home. Rather than let the boy know where he lived, Dickens pretended that a large house over the bridge was his home. He even went up the steps and knocked at the door whilst Bob Fagin watched him out of hearing. When the door was answered he asked if Bob Fagin lived there, which enabled him to get away now that his conductor was out of sight, and proceed to the Marshalsea Prison.

I recollect in the early days of films an excellent attempt at combining real people with cartoons. The particular film I have in mind was called *Out of the Inkpot.* A cartoonist, dipping his pen into some ink, drew the figure of a little clown. The figure became animated, stepped off the paper, slid down the leg of the table and in spite of protests from the real live artist began to perpetrate various acts of mischief about the room. His creator, the artist, had lost control of him and it wasn't until the end of the film that the little cartoon figure was persuaded to return to the paper. The artist then bent the paper and poured the drawing back into the inkpot.

In a similar way, Fagin, one of the most powerful villains in Dickens, seems to me at times to have taken possession of his creator. When Dickens was approaching the end of the *Oliver* story he wrote to Forster, with whom he had arranged to go out riding: 'I don't ride till tomorrow, not having yet disposed of the Jew who is such an out and outer that I don't know what to make of him.'[19]

In the end he made a wonderful study of him, and anyone wishing to accuse Dickens even in these early days in his literary career of creating flat, or 'cardboard' figures should read Chapter 52, containing the account of Fagin's last night alive, in particular what was passing in his mind as he stood in the dock, noticing trivial things—an artist breaking his pencil point, a missing railing spike; he whispers while he listens to the judge pronouncing the death sentence, 'an old man—an old man—an old man' and trails away into silence.

The boys of the gang all make their mark to a lesser

extent. The Artful Dodger, a sort of Sam Weller who has gone wrong, almost excites the reader's sympathy with his perkiness and cheek even in adversity. Noah Claypole, alias Morris Bolter, a later member of the gang, was a very despicable character (also the subject of a printer's error, his name in Chapter 42 being spelt Dolter).[20] Forster mentions one occasion when at Doughty Street one evening Dickens discussed with him what was to be the fate of the boys, and how Serjeant Talfourd had pleaded eloquently for Charley Bates and also the Artful Dodger. Bates, who turned on Sikes at last, reformed and became a grazier in Northamptonshire, but the Dodger, in spite of Talfourd's advocacy, was transported.

Dickens was constantly in touch with the artist about the illustrations and when possible sent Cruikshank the script from which to choose his subjects. The author, however, often suggested suitable subjects himself; in October 1837 he recommended 'Oliver's reception by Fagin and the boys'. The result was a sketch of some lively action—even Sikes was depicted smiling on that occasion. Sometimes the script was not ready to be sent to the artist, in which case Dickens set out in detail what was needed—a *small* kettle for one on the fire, a *small* black teapot on the table with a little tray and so forth, and a two-ounce tin tea canister; also a shawl hanging up—and the cat and kittens before the fire. This was setting the scene indeed for 'Mr Bumble and Mrs Corney taking tea'.[21] All these instructions were faithfully carried out by the illustrator.

On another occasion Dickens thought, after writing it, that the scene of Sikes's escape would not do for illustration being so very complicated, with such a multitude of figures, such violent action, and all by torchlight, that it could hardly be depicted on a small plate.[22] But Cruikshank did illustrate this scene, despite Dickens's expressed opinion, and quite successfully. He eliminated the crowd by taking a high viewpoint, and having to deal with just a few spectators at lighted windows, with a foreground view of Sikes and the door on the roof, and night-time depicted quite effectively.

Dickens was in Liverpool when the plates for the third volume of *Oliver Twist* were being prepared. On seeing them, he wrote to the artist:

With reference to the last one—Rose Maylie and Oliver, without entering into the question of great haste, or any other cause, which may have led to its being what it is—I am quite sure there can be little difference of opinion between us with respect to the result. May I ask you whether you will object to designing this plate afresh, and doing so *at once* in order that as few impressions as possible of the present one may go forth? I feel confident you know me too well to feel hurt by this enquiry, and with equal confidence in you, I have lost no time in preferring it.[23]

Apparently the artist tried at first to improve the original plate, but Dickens was not happy with the result and Cruikshank replaced it with another of Rose Maylie and Oliver in the church.[24] The author very quickly returned to London in case any other alterations were necessary. According to Forster's letter to Bentley, much more needed doing. In pointing out to Bentley that certain plates must be omitted he said: 'I allude to Mr Cruickshank's [*sic*] plate at pp. 216 and 313. The others of the third volume are bad enough but these must not really be allowed to remain an instant.' Although Dickens had only mentioned one to Cruikshank, Forster intimated that he had great difficulty in prevailing upon Dickens to restrict the omissions to only two. 'Lose no moment,' he wrote, 'in getting rid of "Sykes [*sic*] attempting to destroy his dog" (qy—tail-less baboon) —and "Rose Maylie and Oliver"—long known as a Rowland Macasser frontispiece to a sixpenny book of forfeits.'[25] One wonders why the drawings provoked such strong language on the part of Forster. Although the last plate was replaced in subsequent copies of *Oliver*, the 'tail-less baboon' was allowed to remain. Maybe Dickens was more concerned about Rose Maylie than Sikes's dog.

Sikes is quite a striking creation, whose qualities of ignorance and brutishness are played upon by Fagin. Fagin, Sikes and Nancy form the great trio of characters in *Oliver Twist*. That was appreciated by Sir Herbert Tree when he presented his famous production of that book, casting himself as Fagin, Lyn Harding as Sikes—possibly the best of all Sikeses, and Constance Collier as Nancy. Dickens of course realized their importance when he cast himself for these three great parts in his reading of the murder, which played such havoc with his health. At Doughty Street, he had already tried its effect upon an audience: 'Hard at work still. Nancy is no more. I showed what I have done to Kate last night, who was in an unspeakable "*state*"; from which and my own impression I augur well.' (Poor Kate!) 'When I have sent Sikes to the Devil, I must have yours.'[26] Again Dickens's curious taste for the macabre, again the fat boy's wish—'I wants to make your flesh creep!' Thirty years later Dickens was to write to his daughter describing the effect on an audience of his reading of the murder of Nancy:

At Clifton, on Monday night, we had a contagion of fainting. And yet the place was not hot. I should think we had from a dozen to twenty ladies borne out, stiff and rigid, at various times. It became quite ridiculous.[27]

Nonetheless, Dickens obviously enjoyed the power he could wield over his audience.

In writing about Sikes, Dickens was remembering his visits to Sunbury, when he was eighteen, and so was able to describe so accurately the route taken by the burglar through Hampton, past the 'Red Lion', which still stands, along the river road, past the church at Sunbury, where the clock struck seven, with its yew trees overhanging the graves, and the light of the ferry house shining across the road. The old yew trees are still flourishing—threatened occasionally, but still stirring gently in the night wind.[28] Having walked over Sikes's route, I have a great respect for his walking powers which must have been akin to those of his creator. At Chertsey is Pyrcroft House, said to be the one Dickens had in mind for the Maylies' house—now a primary school—and at the Doughty Street Museum is the small window from that house, through which Oliver was said to have been pushed by the burglar. A boy who never existed being put through a window by a man who never existed! But visitors to Doughty Street love that window and almost believe in it—such is the power of Dickens's fiction.

For the flight of Sikes after the murder, Dickens drew upon his recent experience of North End, Hampstead. The route can still be quite easily followed, as I have done on several occasions:

He went through Islington; strode up the hill at Highgate on which there stands the stone in honour of Whittington; turned down Highgate Hill, unsteady of purpose, and uncertain where to go; struck off to the right again, almost as soon as he began to descend it; and taking the footpath across the fields, skirted Caen Wood [now Kenwood] and so came out on Hampstead Heath. Traversing the hollow by the Vale of Health, he mounted the opposite bank, and crossing the road which joins the villages of Hampstead and Highgate, made along the remaining portion of the heath to the fields at North End, in one of which he laid himself down under a hedge, and slept.[29]

Dickens, less than a year before, had rested here himself, in Collins's Farm, after the death of Mary Hogarth.

It is interesting to contemplate the ease with which Dickens wrote in those days: there were few corrections to the manuscript, written in a fairly large and clear hand, as compared with the much smaller handwriting and very much amended manuscript of his later career. Henry Burnett, his brother-in-law, called one evening at Doughty Street and has left a most interesting account of Dickens's manner of working:

> One night in Doughty Street, Mrs Charles Dickens, my wife and myself were sitting round the fire cosily enjoying a chat, when Dickens, for some purpose, came suddenly into the room. 'What, you here!' he exclaimed; 'I'll bring down my work.' It was his monthly portion of Oliver Twist for Bentley's. In a few moments he returned, manuscript in hand, and while he was pleasantly discoursing he employed himself in carrying to a corner of the room a little table, at which he seated himself and recommenced his writing. We, at his bidding, went on talking our 'little nothings', he every now and then (the feather of his pen still moving rapidly from side to side), put in a cheerful interlude. It was interesting to watch, upon the sly, the mind and the muscles working (or, if you please, playing) in company as new thoughts were being dropped upon the paper. And to note the working brow, the set of mouth, with the tongue tightly pressed against the closed lips, as was his habit.[30]

This in all probability took place in the morning room at the back of the ground floor.

His writing at that time was mixed up with his domestic affairs:

> I was thinking about Oliver till dinner-time yesterday, and just as I had fallen upon him tooth and nail, was called away to sit with Kate. I did eight slips, however, and hope to make them fifteen this morning.[31]

That was at the time of the birth of Mamie, his first daughter.

He was very enthusiastic about this story and even on holiday he had a job to keep away from his work ('I have great difficulty in keeping my hands off Fagin and the rest of them in the evenings; but as I am down for rest, I have resisted the temptation.').[32] Earlier in the year he had found it impossible to invite Bentley to coffee at Doughty Street, as he was 'head over ears with Oliver'.[33]

As he did for all his books, Dickens inscribed many presentation copies of *Oliver* for his friends: J. P. Harley,[34] the actor; Thomas Hill,[35] the book collector, Rev. W. Giles, the Baptist minister who was Dickens's first schoolmaster in Chatham,[36] and first gave the name of The Inimitable Boz to his old pupil; Serjeant Talfourd;[37] Bulwer Lytton;[38] and Edward Chapman, one of his publishing partners, on the fly-leaf of whose copy of *Pickwick Papers* Dickens wrote this reference to *Oliver Twist*:

> 'How should you like to grow up a clever man, and write books?' said the old gentleman.
>
> 'I think I would rather read them, Sir,' replied Oliver.
>
> 'What! Wouldn't you like to be a book writer?' said the old gentleman.
>
> Oliver considered a little while, and at last said he should think it would be a much better thing to be a bookseller; upon which the old gentleman laughed heartily, and declared he had said a very good thing, which Oliver felt glad to have done, though he by no means knew what it was.
>
> Vide Oliver Twist, in which the old gentleman does *not* say, though I *do* that Chapman and Hall are the best of booksellers past, present, or to come; and my trusty friends, which I give under my hand for the benefit of Edward Chapman, his book, this fourteenth day of November, 1839.[39]

There were naturally various piracies published, two of which Dickens called to Bentley's attention. He enclosed the commencing numbers of two piracies of *Oliver* and pointed out that the publishers had put up placards, each one claiming to be the only true edition.[40] The two piracies were *The Life and Adventures of Oliver Twiss, the workhouse boy* by Bos (in 79 weekly parts), with Mumble, Solomons, Jem Blount and the Knowing Cove, and *Oliver Twiss* by

Poz (in 20 parts) with Fumble and Merryberry. The first named is on view at the Dickens House.

As mentioned in Chapter 8, the American publishers Carey, Lea and Blanchard had offered to pay Dickens for the parts of *Pickwick* they had published, and he had declined the offer. However, he did in turn offer to make early proofs of *Oliver* available to them, in an endeavour to beat the pirates. This attempt was unsuccessful, and before Lea and Blanchard's two-volume edition could be published in 1839, a New York edition had already appeared.

In *Oliver Twist*, Dickens had attempted for the first time a plot in a long novel, and by present-day standards the coincidences within the plot are quite extraordinary. That Oliver should be taken in the first place to the house of Mr Brownlow, who knew his mother, and then taken by Bill Sikes to burgle a house quite a distance from London, in which his aunt lived, are rather unlikely happenings. Melodrama in those days was full of such coincidences, however, and they were readily accepted by audiences in the theatre and readers of novels.

In Chapter 34 of *Oliver Twist*, Dickens dwelt at some length on the state of the mind between sleeping, dreaming and waking. Mr G. H. Lewes, a writer and critic who took a great interest in mental phenomena, wrote to him about a passage in *Oliver*. Dickens replied:

> I suppose like most authors I look over what I write with exceeding pleasure and think (to use the words of the elder Mr Weller) 'in my innocence that it's all wery capital.' I thought that passage a good one *when* I wrote it, certainly, and I felt it strongly (as I do almost every word I put on paper) *while* I wrote it, but how it came I can't tell. It came like all my other ideas, such as they are, ready made to the point of the pen—and down it went.[41]

Lewes was already known to Dickens as they had met following the critic's favourable review of *Pickwick Papers* in *The National Magazine and Monthly Critic*. Lewes at the time had been surprised at Dickens's library at Furnival's, which he found consisted of nothing but three-volume novels and books on travel. He formed a different view of Dickens's collection of books when he called on him two years later.

For the first time, Dickens seemed to have become aware that some interest might attach to the manuscript of this novel and he made a somewhat late attempt to collect it. He wrote to Charles Hicks, foreman of the printers Bradbury and Evans, asking him to look up all the old copy as he wanted to have the manuscript complete.[42] Apparently the portion remaining, twenty-two chapters now in the Victoria and Albert Museum, was found at Bentley's office and purchased by Forster in 1870. Half a page of manuscript from Chapter 10 is now at Doughty Street, in the study in which it was originally written.[43] It is a fascinating thought when at 48 to remember all the great characters created in that little house, a friendly place, cared for by people who love it—not a brick and stone memorial, which would have been contrary to the wishes of Dickens, but a permanent reminder of a brilliant young man, making his way in life and beginning to get to the top.

CHAPTER 10

'Here's richness!'

Nicholas Nickleby was contracted for as 'another and new book or work the title whereof has not yet been decided' in an agreement with Chapman and Hall dated 18 November 1837. At that time Dickens was fully occupied with the writing of both *Pickwick Papers* and *Oliver Twist*, and it is unlikely that much planning on the new novel had been done at this early stage.

By 22 September 1838, the date of yet another agreement with Bentley, the next serial for Chapman and Hall had been named. An embargo had been placed upon Dickens in respect of the writing of any work beyond that agreed for Bentley. The agreement stipulated:

> That during the said Editorship [of *Bentley's Miscellany*] the said Charles Dickens shall not edit, conduct or write for any periodical publication whatsoever other than the said Miscellany, and other than and except a work called 'The Pickwick Club', now completed, and publishing by Chapman and Hall, of the Strand, London, Booksellers and Publishers, and a work of similar nature entitled 'The Life and Adventures of Nicholas Nickleby.'[1]

Although he may have turned it over in his mind earlier, it was not until the beginning of 1838 that any definite indication was given in Dickens's correspondence that a subject for the new novel was being contemplated. Then he wrote to Harrison Ainsworth:

> I should have written to you before, but my month's work has been dreadful—Grimaldi, the anonymous book for Chapman and Hall [*Sketches of Young Gentlemen*] Oliver and the Miscellany. They are all done, thank God, and I start on my pilgrimage to the cheap schools of Yorkshire (a mighty secret of course) next Monday morning.[2]

It seems that he had made up his mind to expose these schools in his next novel.

A few days later he was writing to Kate from Greta Bridge, Yorkshire, after a very grim journey through snow-storms (vividly described in Chapters 5 and 6 of *Nickleby*):

> We have had for breakfast, toasts, cakes, a Yorkshire pie, a piece of beef about the size and much the shape of my portmanteau, tea, coffee, ham and eggs—and are now going to look about us. Having finished our discoveries, we start in a postchaise for Barnard Castle which is only four miles off, and there I deliver the letter given me by Mitton's friend.[3]

This letter had been given to Dickens by Charles Smithson, a Yorkshire friend and partner of Mitton. It was addressed to an attorney in Yorkshire, Richard Barnes, and it indicated that Dickens wanted to find a school for the son of a widowed friend.

Richard Barnes, Dickens recollected, was 'a jovial, ruddy, broadfaced man'. After mentioning a school nearby, Barnes seemed to have second thoughts and before leaving said:

> 'Weel, Misther, we've been vary pleasant toogather, and ar'll spak my moind tiv'ee. Dinnot let the weedur send her lattle boy to yan o' our school-measthers while there's a harse to hoold in a' Lunnon or a goother to lie asleep in. Ar wouldn't mak' ill words amang my neeburs, and ar' speak tiv'ee quiet loike. But I'm dom'd if ar can gang to bed and not tellee, for weedur's sak', to keep the lattle boy from a' sik scoundrels while there's a harse to hoold in a' Lunnun, or a goother to lie asleep in!' Repeating these words with great heartiness, and with a solemnity on his jolly face that made it look twice as large as before, he shook hands and went away. I never saw him afterwards, but I sometimes imagine that I descry a faint reflection of him in John Browdie.[4]

So here is an original in *Nickleby* identified by Dickens himself, although some doubt seems to have been thrown upon this because of the age of Richard Barnes.

Dickens wrote with obvious affection for the good-hearted Yorkshireman and it is easy to imagine the great fun he had in writing of the occasion when John Browdie frees Smike from the clutches of Squeers, in London. Having let Smike escape, John Browdie, who was supposed to be ill, got into Mr Squeers's bed once more, and drawing the clothes over his head, laughed till he was nearly smothered. If there could only have been somebody by, to see how the bed-clothes shook, and to see the Yorkshireman's great red face and round head appear above the sheets every now and then, like some jovial monster coming to the surface to breathe, and once more dive down convulsed with the laughter which came bursting forth afresh—that somebody would have been scarcely less amused than John Browdie himself.[5]

Forster, in his biography, says that as the time for beginning *Nickleby* approached, Dickens thought of his promise to produce *Barnaby Rudge* for Bentley in November, and sensed it hanging over him like a hideous nightmare.[6] The writing of *Nickleby* seemed fraught with some difficulty at first. But on his birthday Dickens wrote to Forster, 'I *have* begun! I wrote four slips last night, so you see a beginning is made. And what is more, I can go on!'[7]

Writing to Forster a little later to put off a horse-ride because of bad weather, he suggested a walk instead and said, 'The first chapter of Nickleby is done'.[8] On the next day he told his publishers that he had been decoyed away to the theatre and seduced from Nicholas—'but the first chapter is ready, and I mean (God willing) to begin in earnest tomorrow night'.[9] He was still cancelling his riding in March because of the necessity of tackling *Nickleby*.[10] By 8 March, the writing of the book was still not going well, but on that day he started early and wrote twenty slips, leaving only four to do.[11] By the end of the month the first number was published, after the proofs had been re-set.

Dickens went away to Richmond to be out of town when the first number appeared, something he tried to do with most of his books. He stayed with Kate, who was not very well, at the 'Star and Garter' on Richmond Hill, where they were joined by Forster, celebrating his birthday and their wedding anniversary together. This became an annual celebration for twenty years, and was always held at the 'Star and Garter', except when Dickens was abroad.[12]

In the May number two short stories were introduced, told at the inn at Grantham by travellers, after the accident to the coach. Possibly Dickens was short of material, having advanced the main plot as far as he intended that month. He explained to Forster that he still had five slips to fill and he did not know what to put in them.[13] The two stories, 'The Five Sisters of York' and 'The Baron of Grogzwig', were the last interpolated tales he introduced into long novels. 'The Five Sisters of York', a story relating to the famous window in York Minster, no doubt remained in his mind from his visit during his tour in Yorkshire earlier in the year.[14]

A printer's error in Part Four of *Nickleby* ('visitor' for 'sister') was uncorrected in the first issues, and is therefore now one of the indications of a first edition.[15]

The quality of food was often very poor and little supervision was exercised to protect the consumer. Until well after the middle of the nineteenth century, watering the milk or removing its fat content were very common practices.[16] Milk was quite expensive, and Dickens was often topical in his references to such matters—as, for example, in *Nickleby*, when Mr Squeers orders two-penny-worth of milk for the five boys at the 'Saracen's Head', Snow Hill, London.

> 'This is two penn'orth of milk is it, waiter?' said Mr Squeers, looking down into a large blue mug, and slanting it gently so as to get an accurate view of the quantity of liquid contained in it.
>
> 'That's two penn'orth, Sir,' replied the waiter.
>
> 'What a rare article milk is, to be sure, in London!' said Mr Squeers with a sigh. 'Just fill that mug up with lukewarm water, William, will you?'
>
> 'To the very top, Sir?' inquired the waiter. 'Why, the milk will be drownded.'
>
> 'Never you mind that,' replied Mr Squeers. 'Serve it right for being so dear.'[17]

It is typical of Dickens to impart interesting information in a humorous way. In an unpublished autobiographical fragment, he relates that when, as a boy, he worked in Warren's Blacking Warehouse, and walked to work from Camden Town:

> I was so young and childish, and so little qualified—how could I be otherwise?—to undertake the whole charge of my own existence, that in going to Hungerford Stairs of a morning, I could not resist the stale pastry put out at half price on trays at the confectioners' doors in Tottenham Court Road; and I often spent in that, the money I should have kept for my dinner.[18]

This piece of autobiography is again reflected in *Nickleby* when Squeers brings his son Wackford to London and introduces him to Ralph Nickleby. After remarking on his fatness and firmness of flesh, Squeers borrows two pence from Ralph, which he hands to his son, saying: 'Here! You go and buy a tart—and mind you buy a rich one. Pastry makes his flesh shine a good deal, and parents think that a healthy sign.'[19]

Again, though the advertisement for Dotheboys Hall sounds wildly exaggerated, it is not so far away from the actual facts. Mr Squeers's advertisement runs:

> Education.—At Mr Wackford Squeers's Academy, Dotheboys Hall, at the delightful village of Dotheboys, near Greta Bridge in Yorkshire, Youth are boarded, clothed, booked, furnished with pocket money, provided with all necessaries, instructed in all languages, living and dead, mathematics, orthography, geometry, astronomy, trigonometry, the use of the globes, algebra, single stick (if required), writing, arithmetic, fortification, and every other branch of classical literature. Terms, twenty guineas per annum. No extras, no vacations, and diet unparalleled. Mr Squeers is in town, and attends daily, from one till four, at the Saracen's Head, Snow Hill. N.B. An able assistant wanted. Annual salary £5. A Master of Arts would be preferred.[20]

One of the many real advertisements appearing in the newspapers about 1829 was in *The Times*, and it ran:

> Education by Mr Shaw, at Bowes Academy, Greta Bridge, Yorkshire—YOUTH are carefully instructed in the English, Latin and Greek languages, writing, common and decimal arithmetic, book-keeping, mensuration, surveying, geometry and navigation with the most useful branches of the mathematics and are provided with board, and every necessary at 20 guineas per annum each. No extra charges whatever, doctors bills excepted. No vacation except by the parents' desire. The French language 2 guineas per annum extra. Further particulars may be known on application to Mr Young, Plough Yard, Crown Street, Soho, or Mr Walker at 27, Drury Lane. Also for further particulars see a card of Mr Shaw who attends daily at the George, Blue Boar, High Holborn from 12 to 2 o'clock. Mr Seaton Agent, 10 Frederick Place, Goswell Street.[21]

It was Mr Shaw who claimed the rather dubious honour of being the original of Mr Squeers. Shaw certainly had one eye, and the description of Squeers states:

He had but one eye, and the popular prejudice runs in favour of two. The eye he had was unquestionably useful, but decidedly not ornamental, being of a greenish grey, and in shape resembling the fan-light of a street door.[22]

(The fan-light is still over the street door at Doughty Street, an example of the technique Dickens used to get across his vivid descriptions.) Yet another real advertisement, by a Mr Horn of Brough Academy, near Greta Bridge, Yorkshire, contained a similar syllabus. Fanciful as it sounds, therefore, Mr Squeers's syllabus was quite within the bounds of truth. Dickens received a letter about this subject from Lord Robert Grosvenor, son of the first Marquis of Westminster, enclosing a cutting of a similar advertisement in *The Times* lodged by a Mr Twycross. In thanking him, Dickens pointed out that he had been in Mr Twycross's neighbourhood during his previous winter's tour in Yorkshire.[23]

The American publishers Carey, Lea and Blanchard were again in touch with Dickens giving him the welcome news that *Nickleby* was very popular in America. Dickens regretted he had been unable to supply their request for early proofs, because he had been behind-hand rather than in advance in writing the instalments. Strange to say, the writing of *Nickleby* seemed to give him more difficulty than other books, and he wrote to Macready that although he compelled himself to work first at *Nickleby*, he found he could not write as quickly as usual.[24] And to Forster he wrote in a Jingle-like fashion: 'I have just begun my second chapter (Ch. 31); cannot go out to-night; must get on—think there *will* be a Nickleby at the end of this month now (I doubted it before).'[25] One rather wonders at this, because by this time the story was well advanced, and Nicholas was on his way back to London to save his sister.

Excluding the letters he wrote while he was away on holiday on various business trips, Dickens wrote over 550 letters from Doughty Street between April 1837 and December 1839—that is, letters that have been traced and published. During that period, however, he wrote one letter which does not appear in this collection and which is not even in his name. It is certainly an outstanding letter and is worth recalling here. It is the one he wrote for Fanny Squeers from Dotheboys Hall to Nicholas's uncle, Ralph

Nickleby, to describe the hero's assault upon her father.

No audience ever fails to respond to its recital, and I find that during my many talks on Dickens I have repeated it over a thousand times, since I gave it first to the Dickens Fellowship's Leyton branch in 1946. Modern universities in California, and ancient ones in Heidelburg, colleges, schools, literary societies and more universities throughout America, Norway, Sweden, Denmark, Finland, Germany, Switzerland, France and Holland, all nationalities and all ages appreciate and enjoy it alike. It is a wonderful piece of humorous writing, and must have contributed a great deal towards the popularity of *Nicholas Nickleby*.

> Dotheboys Hall,
> Thursday Morning
>
> Sir,
>
> My pa requests me to write to you. The doctors considering it doubtful whether he will ever recuvver the use of his legs which prevents his holding a pen.
>
> We are in a state of mind beyond everything, and my pa is one mask of brooses both blue and green likewise two forms are steepled in his Goar. We were kimpelled to have him carried down into the kitchen where he now lays. You will judge from this that he has been brought very low.
>
> When your nevvew that you recommended for a teacher had done this to my pa and jumped upon his body with his feet and also langwedge which I will not pollewt my pen with describing, he assaulted my ma with dreadful violence, dashed her to the earth, and drove her back comb several inches into her head. A very little more and it must have entered her skull. We have a medical certifiket that if it had, the torter-shell would have affected the brain.
>
> Me and my brother were then the victims of his feury since which we have suffered very much which leads us to the arrowing belief that we have received some injury in our insides, especially as no marks of violence are visible externally. I am screaming out loud all the time I write and so is my brother which takes off my attention rather, and I hope you will excuse mistakes.
>
> The monster having satiated his thirst for blood ran away, taking with him a boy of desperate caracter that he excited to rebellyon, and a garnet ring belonging to my ma, and not having been apprehended by the constables is supposed to have been took up by some stage-coach. My pa begs that if he comes to you the ring may be returned, and that you will let the thief and assassin go, as if we prosecuted him he would only be transported, and if he is let go he is sure to be hung before long,

which will save us trouble, and be much more satisfactory. Hoping to
hear from you when convenient

I remain

Yours and cetrer

Fanny Squeers

P.S. I pity his ignorance and despise him.[26]

The piece of manuscript containing this letter has come
to rest in London, in the British Museum. As Mr Squeers so
aptly said, 'Here's richness!'

William Hastings Hughes, five-year-old brother of
Richard, the author of *Tom Brown's Schooldays*, was shown
by his father the pictures in *Nicholas Nickleby* and had the
story told to him as far as it had progressed. He was disappointed that Nicholas and the boys had not been re-
warded, nor had Squeers and his family been punished. His
father told him that Dickens might be persuaded to alter
the ending if he was written to, and so Master Hughes had a
letter written for him.[27] This was sent to Dickens through a
friend of the family, the Rev. R. H. Barham. Dickens was
very amused to get this letter and although he was very busy
at the time, took great trouble in replying to Master
Hughes:

Doughty Street, London,

Twelfth December 1838.

Respected Sir,

I have given Squeers one cut on the neck and two on the head, at
which he appeared much surprised and began to cry, which, being a
cowardly thing, is just what I should have expected from him—wouldn't
you?

I have carefully done what you told me in your letter about the lamb
and the two 'sheeps' for the little boys. They have also had some good
ale and porter, and some wine. I am sorry you didn't say *what* wine
you would like them to have. I gave them some sherry which they liked
very much, except one boy, who was a little sick and choked a good deal.
He was rather greedy, and that's the truth, and I believe it went the
wrong way, which I say served him right, and I hope you will say so,
too.

Nicholas had his roast lamb as you said he was to, but he could not eat
it all, and says if you do not mind his doing so he should like to have the
rest hashed tomorrow with some greens, which he is very fond of, and
so am I. He said he did not like to have his porter hot, for he thought it
spoilt the flavour, so I let him have it cold. You should have seen him

drink it. I thought he never would have left off. I also gave him three pounds of money, all in sixpences, to make it seem more, and he said directly that he should give more than half to his mamma and sister, and divide the rest with poor Smike. And I say he is a good fellow for saying so; and if anybody says he isn't I am ready to fight him whenever they like—there!

Fanny Squeers shall be attended to, depend upon it. Your drawing of her is very like, except that I don't think the hair is quite curly enough. The nose is particularly like hers, and so are the legs. She is a nasty disagreeable thing, and I know it will make her very cross when she sees it; and what I say is that I hope it may. You will say the same I know—at least I think you will.

I meant to have written you a long letter, but I cannot write very fast when I like the person I am writing to, because that makes me think about them, and I like you, and so I tell you. Besides, it is just eight o'clock at night, and I always go to bed at eight o'clock, except when it is my birthday, and then I sit up to supper. So I will not say anything more besides this—and that is my love to you and Neptune; and if you will drink my health every Christmas Day, I will drink yours—come.

I am, Respected Sir,

Your affectionate friend.

P.S. I don't write my name very plain, but you know what it is you know, so never mind.[28]

This reply was sent via the Rev. Barham to whom Dickens wrote:

Accept a thousand thanks for the Epistle which found me cogitating the next number of Nicholas, and instantly took me away from it to write an answer, which I inclose. I send it open for your edification, but when you have read it pray seal it with a very large seal, in order that it may bear an appearance of becoming form and gravity. The communication to which it is a reply, has amused me highly.[29]

A Mrs S. C. Hall, a writer and editor of many journals, wrote to Dickens calling attention to a case against a Yorkshire schoolmaster, which the author had already noted. In his reply he said that the rascalities of those Yorkshire schoolmasters could not be easily exaggerated, and that he had kept down the strong truth and thrown as much comicality over it as he could, rather than disgust the reader with its fouler aspects. Dickens pointed out that he saw the identical scoundrel she referred to, his name being Shaw. In addition to the action referred to in the newspaper cutting, Dickens also thought that another action had been brought against Shaw by the parent of a miserable child, a cancer in whose head Shaw had opened with an inky penknife, and so caused his death.[30]

Dickens was apparently mistaken in his last supposition, confusing Shaw with another schoolmaster so accused, and also with a pupil who had admitted that he had used a penknife on himself for such purpose. Dickens makes Squeers say:

> 'Mrs Squeers, Sir, is as she always is—a mother to them lads ... One of our boys gorging hisself with vittles, and then turning ill; that's their way—got a abscess on him last week. To see how she operated upon him with a penknife! O lor! What a member of society that woman is!'[31]

In his preface to *Nickleby*, Dickens says that Squeers is 'the representative of a class and not of an individual—a faint and feeble picture of an existing reality'.

There are records of the case against Shaw in October 1823, brought against him by the parents of a boy named Jones. Jones told his story in court:

> 'There were nearly 300 boys in the school. We had meat three times a week, and on the other days potatoes and bread and cheese. When any gentleman came to see his children, Mr Shaw used to order the boys who were without trousers or jackets to get under the desks; we were sometimes without trousers for four or five days while they were being mended. They boys washed in a long trough similar to what the horses drink from; the boys had but two towels, and the big boys used to take advantage of the little boys, and get the towels first; we had no supper; we had warm water and milk for tea and dry bread; we had hay and straw beds, and one sheet to each bed, in which four or five boys slept; there were about 30 beds in one room, and a large tub in the middle ... we had quills furnished us to flea the beds every morning, and we caught a good beating if we did not fill the quills with fleas; we had the skimmings of the pot every Sunday afternoon; the usher offered a penny for every maggot, and the boys found more than a quart full, but he did not give them the money ... On one occasion (in October) I felt a weakness in my eyes, and could not write my copy; the defendant said he would beat me; on the next day I could not see at all, and I told Mr Shaw, who sent me, with three others to the wash-house; ... those who were totally blind were sent into a room; there were nine boys in this room totally blind; a Mr Benning, a doctor, was sent for ... I was in the room two months, and the doctor then discharged me, saying I had lost one eye; in fact, I was blind with both ...'[32]

Much of the evidence given by the boy was punctuated by laughter! Nevertheless, heavy damages were awarded against Shaw. It seems likely that Dickens saw this report and used some of the material in his chapters about Dotheboys Hall.

In his letter to Mrs Hall, Dickens continued:

> There is an old Church near the school, and the first grave-stone I stumbled on that dreary winter afternoon was placed above the grave of a boy, eighteen long years old, who had died—'suddenly' the inscription said; I suppose his heart broke—the Camel falls down 'suddenly' when they heap the last load upon his back—died in that wretched place. I think his ghost put Smike into my head, upon the spot.[33]

This letter is now on view in the Dickens House Museum. The boy in question was George Ashton Taylor.

On their coach journey to the North, Dickens and his illustrator, Browne, on reaching Grantham met 'a very queer old lady', the Mistress of a Yorkshire school, who showed them a letter she was carrying to a schoolboy from his father. It contained a severe lecture, and quotations from the Scriptures, on the subject of the boy's refusal to eat boiled meat.[34] This undoubtedly inspired the letter to Mobbs, read by Squeers, to the effect that 'Mobbs's mother-in-law took to her bed on hearing that he would not eat fat, and has been very ill ever since'.[35]

In acknowledging some highland whisky he had been sent, Dickens wrote a letter of thanks to the donor in which he pointed out that he would know what had inspired him if the next number of *Nickleby* on which he was working was specially good.[36] The chapters in question (34 to 36) certainly contain some good comedy—the Mantalinis, Squeers in London, Mrs Nickleby being introduced to Smike and another birth in the Kenwigs family, among other events, so maybe the whisky did its work!

It may have been working even better still a month or so later in Part Thirteen, published in April 1839, and containing Chapter 41. 'I think Mrs Nickleby's love scene will come out rather unique',[37] the author wrote to Forster. Mrs Elizabeth Dickens, mother of the novelist, was recalled by Thomas Powell, an early friend of the family, as incoherent in speech and very vain of her wasp-like waist.

Mrs Nickleby has always been accepted as a gentle carica-
ture of Dickens's mother, although presumably she did not
recognize herself when she read the novel. Dickens
mentioned his mother's disbelief in the possibility of such a
character in his letter to Forster from Broadstairs on 11
August 1842. Mrs Nickleby is indeed one of Dickens's
great female characters, though in real life her scatter-
brained twitterings would make her a very exhausting person
to live with. In reference to Frank Cheeryble, Mrs Nickleby
says:

> 'I hope that this unaccountable conduct may not be the beginning of
> his taking to his bed and living thus all his life, like the Thirsty Woman of
> Tutbury or the Cock-Lane Ghost, or some of those extraordinary
> creatures. One of them had some connexion with our family. I forget
> without looking back to some old letters I have upstairs, whether it
> was my great grandfather who went to school with the Cock-Lane
> Ghost, or the Thirsty Woman of Tutbury who went to school with
> my grandmother.'[38]

As suggested in Chapter 5, the original of Miss La
Creevy was thought to be Dickens's aunt, Janet Ross, who
painted a miniature of him when he was eighteen (now in
the Dickens House Museum). Edwin Pugh in his book,
The Dickens Originals, suggests Miss Rose Emma
Drummond as a possibility. She also was a miniature artist,
and she painted a miniature of Dickens on ivory, which he
gave to Kate as an engagement present.

Newman Noggs was said to have been based on Newman
Knott, a broken-down character who called at the office of
the solicitors Blackmore and Ellis, where Dickens was a
young clerk, for the weekly dole of seven shillings which a
relative allowed him. Sydney Smith on one occasion referred
to the eagerness of many ladies to meet Dickens, and even
to be put into his stories; indeed, a certain Lady Charlotte
(presumably Lady Charlotte Lindsay) would gladly marry
Newman Noggs.[39] The original of Nicholas was generally
accepted as being Dickens's brother-in-law, Henry Burnett,
although there were perhaps traces of Dickens himself in
that character, too.

William and Daniel Grant, philanthropical merchants of
Ramsbottom and Manchester, were identified by the author
as originals of the Cheeryble brothers. Dickens and Forster

were introduced by letter to Mr Gilbert Winter of Stock House, Cheetham Hill Road, Manchester and it was through him that they met the Grants. It seems possible that at their house Dickens also saw the original of the Cheerybles' butler, David, in the person of the Grants' butler, Alfred Boot. There were really four Grant brothers —William, Daniel, John and Charles.

Whilst up in the North with Browne, Dickens went to the theatre, and wrote to Kate from the Lion Hotel, Shrewsbury:

> We were at the play last night. It was a bespeak—'The Love Chase', a ballet (with a phenomenon!) divers songs, and 'A Roland for an Oliver'. It is a good theatre, but the actors are very funny. Browne laughed with such indecent heartiness at one point of the entertainment, that the old gentleman in the next box suffered the most violent indignation. The bespeak party occupied two boxes, the ladies were full-dressed and the gentlemen, to a man, in white gloves with flowers in their button holes. It amused us mightily, and was really as like the Miss Snevellicci's bespeak in Nickleby could be.[40]

This refers to Miss Snevellicci's benefit at Portsmouth.[41]

It seems to have been suggested, possibly by Forster, that the Haynes Bayleys, song-writers and dramatists, might have been the originals of Mr and Mrs Wittitterley in *Nicholas Nickleby*.[42]

To absorb the atmosphere of the Hampton Races, where Sir Mulberry Hawk and Lord Verisopht quarrelled, Dickens attended the races while staying at Petersham. 'The little race course at Hampton' is likely to refer to the one at Kempton Park, which is still operating, between Hampton and Sunbury. This was Dickens's third visit to this event, maybe held on several days as it is now. He mentions that they worked much harder than the running horses.[43]

It seems that the copy for the July number, in which this episode of *Nickleby* appears, was lost—Dickens suggested by 'some blackguard coachman'—and he had to rewrite these chapters (Chapters 49 to 51, which constituted Part 16, published in July 1839). Apologizing for the consequent lateness of the copy, he attributed it to 'the immorality of the Richmond coachmen'.[44]

The other great group of characters in *Nickleby* was of course the Crummles family and their theatrical company, who contributed in no small measure to the success of the novel, supplying, as they did, the lighter comedy in the story against the grim comedy of the Squeers episodes (see Chapter 12). Here again, perhaps Dickens was drawing a composite picture from his experience of the theatre, though it is thought that the Crummles were roughly based upon the Davenports, a well-known theatrical family.

No obvious originals have been suggested for the Mantalini family, another delightful creation in the gallery of characters in *Nickleby*. (There were 162 altogether, a great increase on the number in *Oliver Twist*, which was doubtless the reason why Dickens, writing to Laman Blanchard in Philadelphia, referred to his difficulty in winding up so many people.)[45] Mantalini's names for his wife, however—'essential juice of pineapple', 'a little rose in a demnition flower-pot'—are dimly reminiscent of Dickens's nicknames for Kate, when he was writing to her during their courtship—'My ever dearest Mouse', 'My dearest Wig', and even 'Dear Pig'.

Dickens took great care to make sure that the illustrations were accurate, and corresponded well with the descriptions in the text; possibly this accounts for his long association with Browne, lasting twenty-three years, because Browne was quite happy to co-operate with him and did not appear to resent the author's criticism. In regard to the illustration 'A Sudden Recognition unexpected on both sides', which depicts Squeers recapturing Smike in a London Street, Dickens added the following note to the original sketch: 'I don't think Smike is frightened enough or Squeers earnest enough—for my purpose.'[46] The original sketch for this illustration, with Dickens's writing on it, is on view at Doughty Street.

For the illustration 'Great excitement of Miss Kenwigs at the hairdresser's shop', the first one in the August 1839 number, Dickens sent detailed instructions to Browne:

A hairdresser's shop at night—not a dashing one, but a barber's. Morleena Kenwigs on a tall chair having her hair dressed by an under-bred attendant with his hair parted down the middle, and frizzed up into curls at the sides. Another customer, who is being shaved, has just turned his head in the direction of Miss Kenwigs, and she and Newman Noggs (who has brought her there, and has been whiling away the time with an old newspaper), recognise, with manifestations of surprise, and Morleena with emotion, Mr Lillyvick, the collector. Mr Lillyvick's bristly beard expresses great neglect of his person, and he looks very grim and in the utmost despondency.[47]

Browne obviously did not rely solely upon these instructions to draw his sketch, because he included the coalheaver who appeared in the scene, but who was not mentioned in Dickens's note to him.

... there presented himself for shaving, a big, burly, good-humoured coalheaver with a pipe in his mouth, who, drawing his hand across his chin, requested to know when a shaver would be disengaged ... 'You won't get shaved here my man.'[48]

The reception of *Nickleby* was generally quite favourable, and Dickens was by this time being accepted as a writer of unusual talent. Sydney Smith, Canon of St Paul's, in a letter to Sir George Philips in September 1838 said: 'Nickleby is very good.' Though he had stood out against him as long as he could, Dickens had conquered him.[49] *The Edinburgh Review* referred to him as the most popular writer of his day, very original, well entitled to his popularity and not likely to lose it. It compared him favourably with the painter Hogarth. What Hogarth was to painting, such very nearly was Mr Dickens in prose fiction.[50] Dickens wrote to Forster thanking him for two copies of the *Sun* newspaper dated 4 July 1839, which contained a review of Part Sixteen of *Nickleby*, referring to it as one of the best instalments, if not the best, of this story, and comparing Dickens favourably with Fielding.[51] This part contained the sequel to the courtship of Mrs Nickleby by the gentleman next door and the fatal duel between Sir Mulberry Hawk and Lord Verisopht. Piracies were of course published, as they had been of the previous books, and it was probably Thomas Peckett Prest, who called himself 'Bos', who brought out *Nickelas Nickelbery*. Although the piracy of *Pickwick Papers* had run for 112 weekly instalments, the *Nickleby* piracy concluded after about ten monthly instalments, with the discovery that Roger Nickelbery had concealed a will which made Smike heir to a fortune.[52]

Dickens made a protest when publishing *Nickleby* against the stealing of authors' works, first by the issue of a leaflet and then by a newspaper advertisement. In *Nickleby* itself he again pointed to this custom, this time ironically, by making Mr Gregsbury, M.P., express the opinion that he would oppose 'any preposterous bill' giving 'poor grubbing devils of authors a right to their own property'.[53] He also protested against dramatizations made without the author's permission.

There were of course more presentation copies than ever, as Dickens enlarged his circle of friends and business connections. Copies were inscribed and given to Harley, the actor, Thomas Hill, the book collector, Leigh Hunt, Maclise, Charles Young, Macready, Dr John Elliotson, Mrs George Cattermole, Samuel Rogers, Albany Fonblanque, editor of *The Examiner*, and Lady Holland. Dickens asked the last named 'to accept from me a copy of Nickleby in a dress which will wear better than his every day clothes'.[54] In dedicating a special copy to Macready, the author wrote:

> The book, the whole book, and nothing but the book (except the binding which is an important item) has arrived at last, and is forwarded herewith. The red represents my blushes at its gorgeous dress; the gilding, all those bright professions which I do not make to you; and the book itself, my whole heart for twenty months, which should be yours for so short a term, as you have it always.[55]

This presentation copy is now in the Dickens House Museum.

Again, as in the case of *Oliver Twist*, Dickens made an attempt to collect the manuscript, and he wrote to the foreman printer, Charles Hicks, of Bradbury and Evans asking him to look for the old manuscript.[56] Apparently, as with *Oliver*, the attempt was not very successful. Only six chapters of *Nickleby* manuscript exist, one of which is at Doughty Street, where it was originally written.

A celebration dinner was held at the 'Albion', Aldersgate Street, which was attended by Forster, Cattermole, Charles Hicks, Thomas Hill, Stanfield, Beard, Maclise, and Sir David Wilkes. Maclise had painted a portrait of Dickens which Thackeray considered to be an exceptionally good one: he thought it 'perfectly amazing; a looking glass could not render a better facsimile'.[57] Dickens wanted to pay Maclise for it, but the artist returned his cheque.[58] The portrait was eventually presented to Dickens by Chapman and Hall at this celebration dinner. It is known as the *Nickleby* portrait because it was used, and is still used, as a frontispiece to the book. The original is in the National Portrait Gallery.

Dickens seemed to find constant difficulty in finishing each part of the story. He found February 1839 a short month in which to get everything done, but by the 22nd he said: 'Nickleby is finished—and (I think) as good a number as the last.'[59] It was late, of course; the agreement had stipulated that the copy should be with the printer on 15 February, which Dickens had failed to accomplish.[60]

Forster was seeing practically all of Dickens's work by the time *Nickleby* came to an end. Proofs of the final numbers were to be sent to him and the author suggested that they devote an evening to a careful reading.[61]

'The discovery is made' (that Ralph Nickleby was Smike's father), 'Ralph is dead, the loves have come all right, Tim Linkinwater has proposed, and I have now only to break up Dotheboys and the book together,' he wrote to Forster.[62] The writing of the book was actually completed at Broadstairs. In his diary dated Friday, 20 September 1839, he recorded: 'Finished Nickleby this day at 2 o'clock and went over to Ramsgate with Fred and Kate to send the last little chapter to Bradbury and Evans in a parcel. Thank God that I have lived to get through it happily.'[63]

CHAPTER 11

Out of town

AFTER moving to Doughty Street, Dickens's first journey of any distance was to North End, Hampstead, where he and his wife spent some weeks at Collins's Farm to recover from the shock of Mary Hogarth's sudden death in May 1837. His first letter from that address was to Thomas Beard and in it he recounted the tragic events of the previous Saturday.[1]

Collins's Farm, on the side of Hampstead Heath, was known earlier as Wylde's Farm, a name which has since been reintroduced. John Collins and his sons were dairy farmers and were probably sub-tenants of a Mr Price. In 1823 Collins sub-let part of the farm to John Linnell, the painter, who in the following year made it his permanent abode and was visited there by the artists Morland, Constable and Blake. A year or so later Linnell added a lean-to kitchen, built with his own hands. The following year, owing to a breakdown in his health, he moved to Bayswater. Collins and Mr Sharman after him continued to let one end of the house, which had been arranged as a cottage with a separate entrance.

A number of well-known people became tenants—Chief Justice Denman, Lord Huntingtower, Colonel Barnes (Secretary of the Garrick Club) and a misogynist named Bromley, who lived there with his manservant and would not allow a petticoat within the house. Artists and literary men lived there from time to time and no doubt Dickens learned of its availability from one of his acquaintances.

Near by is the 'Bull and Bush', celebrated in the old music-hall song, but long before that the haunt of many well-known personalities. Originally said to have been the country seat of Hogarth, the painter, it later became a

'House of Refreshment and Ease', and was frequented by Reynolds, Gainsborough, Sterne, Garrick, Macready and Kean. Addison and Steele, Lamb, Coleridge, Cibber, Foote and Hone were also frequent visitors to 'this delightful little snuggery', as Gainsborough termed it.

An amusing story used to be told about Hone and Lamb. One night, after refreshing themselves in the 'Bull and Bush', they began to moralize on the evils of snuff-taking, and resolving to abandon this habit, both threw away their snuff boxes. Next morning Lamb reconsidered his resolution and returned to the Heath to search in the thickets for his snuff box. He found Hone doing the very same thing. They both recovered their snuff boxes and repaired to the 'Bull and Bush' to celebrate.

William Hone was author of *The Every Day Book* and his works were often illustrated by Cruikshank. Some years later when Hone was dying, he sent the artist to ask Dickens to come and see him. Having read no books of late other than those of Dickens, he wanted to shake hands with the author before he died.[2] A few months later, Dickens attended his funeral, which he described in his own inimitable manner in a letter to C. C. Felton, an American friend:

> You know Hone's book I daresay. Ah! I saw a scene of mingled comicality and seriousness at his funeral some weeks ago, which has choked me at dinner-time ever since. Cruikshank and I went as mourners; and as he lived, poor fellow, five miles out of town, I drove Cruikshank down. It was such a day as I hope, for the credit of nature, is seldom seen in any parts but there—muddy, foggy, wet, dark, cold, and unutterably wretched in every possible respect. Now, Cruikshank has enormous whiskers, which straggle all down his throat in such weather, and stick out in front of him, like a partially unravelled bird's-nest; so that he looks queer enough at the best, but when he is very wet, and in a state between jollity (he is always very jolly with me) and the deepest gravity (going to a funeral, you know), it is utterly impossible to resist him; especially as he makes the strangest remarks the mind of man can conceive, without intention of being funny, but rather meaning to be philosophical. I really cried with an irresistible sense of his comicality all the way, but when he was dressed out in a black cloak and a very long black hatband by an undertaker (who, as he whispered me with tears in his eyes—for he had known Hone for many years—was a 'character and he would like to sketch him'), I thought I should have been obliged to go away. However, we went into a little parlour where

the funeral party was, and God knows it was miserable enough, for the widow and children were crying bitterly in one corner ...

Dickens continued, describing a loud-voiced clergyman (the Rev. Thomas Binney) who was officiating and who, without knowing the author was Cruikshank, criticized to his face a paragraph written about Hone.

> I was really penetrated with sorrow for the family, but when Cruikshank (upon his knees, and sobbing for the loss of an old friend) whispered me, 'that if it wasn't a clergyman, and it wasn't a funeral, he'd have punched his head,' I felt as if nothing but convulsions could possibly relieve me ...[3]

Dickens always had a keen sense of the ludicrous and, as shown in Chapter 2, was not slow to express his contempt of any ostentatious display at funerals.

While Dickens was staying at North End, no doubt on his walks he exercised that photographic memory of his and made himself familiar with that part of the Heath which he was to use shortly afterwards in both *Pickwick Papers* and *Oliver Twist*. He used this knowledge in describing the flight of Sikes from London after the murder, and his sleeping beneath a hedge in the fields at North End, where Collins's Farm is situated. During this time he must have become acquainted with some of the inhabitants of the village, and when he found it necessary to put his father out of reach of his creditors, whilst coming to some arrangement with them, he was able to place John Dickens temporarily with a Mrs Davis, at North End.

On his return to Doughty Street, Dickens was to write the Fleet Prison chapters of *Pickwick* and doubtless in his walks around Collins's Farm he would have become familiar with the nearby Spaniards Inn, which he was to use as the scene of Mrs Bardell's arrest. The incident is preceded by an amusing picnic, attended by Mr and Mrs Raddle, Mrs Cluppins, Mrs Sanders and Mrs Rogers, accompanied of course by Mrs Bardell and Tommy. Mr Raddle has managed several times, on the way, to curry the disfavour of the ladies, and does not improve matters on their arrival at the Spaniards:

> Mr Raddle's very first act nearly occasioned his good lady a relapse; it being neither more nor less than to order tea for seven; whereas (as

the ladies one and all remarked) what could have been easier than for
Tommy to have drank out of anybody's cup—or everybody's, if that
was all—when the waiter wasn't looking: which would have saved one
head of tea, and the tea just as good.[4]

In two letters to Harrison Ainsworth, telling him about
Mary Hogarth, Dickens recalled that his house was not far
away and expressed the hope that he would call on them.[5]
Whilst Kate remained at Hampstead, Dickens returned to
Doughty Street most evenings to attend to any necessary
business.

Collins's Farm was not far from Jack Straw's Castle, to
which Dickens was to ride on a number of occasions, with
Forster and other friends. It was to this hostelry he referred
when he wrote to Forster:

> You don't feel disposed, do you, to muffle up, and start off with me for
> a good brisk walk over Hampstead Heath? I knows a good 'ouse where
> we can have a red hot chop for dinner, and a glass of good wine.[6]

'This,' said Forster, 'led to our first experience of Jack
Straw's Castle'.[7]

In July 1837, Dickens, Kate and Browne went for a
week's holiday in Europe, intending to tour Belgium. He
wrote to Forster on his arrival at the Hotel Rignolle,
Calais:

> We arrived here in great state this morning—I very sick, and Missis
> very well. Just as the boat was leaving Dovor [*sic*], a breathless boots
> put a letter from town, and The Examiner into my hands, the latter
> of which, I verily believe preserved me from that dismal extremity of
> qualmishness into which I am accustomed to sink when I have 'the
> blue above and the blue below'. I have always thought that the 'silence
> wheresoe'er I go' is a beautiful touch of Barry Cornwall's [otherwise
> B. W. Procter] description of the depression produced by sea voyaging.
> I know it's remarkably silent wherever I go, when I am on the briny . . .[8]

Dickens was quoting from 'The Sea' in B. W. Procter's
English Songs (1832).[9] *The Examiner* contained Forster's
review of Part Fifteen of *Pickwick* (the Fleet Prison chapters)
and being very favourable naturally cheered Dickens up.

They had arranged for a post coach to take them to
Ghent, Brussels and Antwerp, among other places. In the
afternoon, they went in a barouche to some gardens where
people were dancing, and 'footing it most heartily—

especially the women who in their short petticoats and light caps looked uncommonly agreeable'. Dickens assuredly had an eye for an ankle! He described a gentleman 'in a blue surtout and silken Berlins' who accompanied them and acted as curator, and even waltzed to show them how it ought to be done. On ringing for their slippers after they returned to their hotel, it turned out that this gentleman was the 'boots' mentioned in the letter to Forster. Dickens promised to see Forster as soon as his sea-sickness had disappeared.[10]

He also wrote to Bentley on a matter relating to *Oliver Twist*. This was presumably Dickens's first visit abroad, though he writes with some authority about sea-sickness and the effect of the sea on him. He had of course been down to the Thames estuary by water and wrote very amusingly on the subject in his short tale 'The Steam Excursion', in *Sketches by Boz*.

Whilst at Doughty Street, Dickens became acquainted with the attractive little seaside resort of Broadstairs, and began an association which lasted almost without a break until 1851, with a later visit in 1859. He stayed first in quite humble lodgings at 12 High Street (later re-numbered 31, but now demolished for road-widening), a road which leads down a steep hill to the sea front. A plaque marks the approximate position of the dwelling, though the actual spot would be somewhere towards the middle of the present road. Before leaving London, Dickens had apparently made up the contents of the next number of *Bentley's Miscellany*, even to advising Cruikshank which would be the best subjects for his illustrations. All this he told to Bentley's chief clerk and accountant, E. S. Morgan, in his first letter from Broadstairs,[11] but he had still to write Part Eighteen of *Pickwick*.

On the same day (3 September 1837) he wrote to Forster saying that he had just risen from an 'attack of illness', though he does not mention what had been the matter, only that he was much better, and hoped to begin writing *Pickwick*—Part Eighteen—the next day:

> You will imagine how queer I must have been when I tell you that I have been compelled for four and twenty mortal hours to abstain from porter or other malt liquor!!! I done it though—really ... I have

discovered that the landlord of the Albion (James Ballard) has delicious hollands (but what is that to *you*, for you cannot sympathise with my feelings), and that a cobbler who lives opposite to my bedroom window is a Roman Catholic, and gives an hour and a half to his devotions every morning behind his counter. I have walked upon the sands at low-water from this place to Ramsgate, and sat upon the same at high-ditto till I have been flayed with the cold. I have seen ladies and gentle-men walking upon the earth in slippers of buff, and pickling themselves in the sea in complete suits of the same. I have seen stout gentlemen looking at nothing through powerful telescopes for hours, and when at last they saw a cloud of smoke, fancying a steamer behind it, and going home comfortable and happy. I have found out that our next neighbour has a wife and something else under the same roof with the rest of the furniture—the wife deaf and blind, and the something else given to drinking...[12]

Some of the impressions collected then were probably recalled when, fourteen years later, he contributed an article to *Household Words* called 'Our English Watering Place':

You would hardly guess which is the main street of our watering place, but you may know it by its being always stopped up with donkey-chaises. Whenever you come here and see harnessed donkeys eating clover out of barrows drawn completely across a narrow thoroughfare, you may be quite sure you are in our High Street.

Little phrases in his paper, written over a hundred and twenty years ago still apply: ... 'a brown litter of tangled seaweed and fallen cliff which looks as if a family of giants had been making tea here for ages, and had observed an untidy custom of throwing their tea-leaves on the shore'; and 'this pretty little semi-circular sweep of houses tapering off at the end of the wooden pier into a point in the sea.'[13]

It was in 1836 that Dickens wrote the short story called 'The Tuggses at Ramsgate', an amusing tale of a journey by boat to the seaside resort between Broadstairs and Pegwell Bay. It makes one wonder whether Dickens saw anything of Ramsgate while he was a boy at Chatham or later during his newspaper career, though no record of such a visit or visits survives today. On this occasion, Dickens's stay in Broad-stairs was quite a brief one—no more than a week. His visit was cut even shorter by a return to town, to which he refers in two letters, necessitated by a burglary at Doughty Street.

He does not give details, but merely indicates that the loss was 'to no very great amount I am happy to say'.[14]

Towards the end of the year (1837) Dickens and Kate, feeling in need of another break, went for a short spell to Brighton, where they stayed at the Old Ship Hotel, which still exists (somewhat extended). Dickens was disappointed that Forster was not able to join them and describes for him an unusually windy day:

> It is a beautiful day and we have been taking advantage of it, but the wind until to-day has been so high and the weather so stormy that Kate has been scarcely able to peep out of doors. On Wednesday it blew a perfect hurricane, breaking windows, knocking down shutters, carrying people off their legs, blowing the fires out, and causing universal consternation. The air was for some hours darkened with a shower of black hats (second hand) which are supposed to have been blown off the heads of unwary passengers in remote parts of the town, and to have been industriously picked up by the fishermen. Charles Kean [second son of Edmund Kean] was advertised for Othello, 'for the benefit of Mrs Sefton, having most kindly postponed for this one day his departure for London'. I have not heard whether he got to the theatre, but I am sure nobody else did. They do The Honeymoon to-night, on which occasion I mean to patronise the drayma.
>
> We have a beautiful bay-windowed sitting room here, fronting the sea, but I have seen nothing of B's [Beard's] brother who was to have shewn me the lions, and my notions of the place are consequently somewhat confined: being limited to the pavilion, the chain-pier and the sea. The last is quite enough for me ...[15]

This letter, with its reference to the shower of hats, is typical of Dickens, such exaggerated description being the means by which he was able to put a fact over humorously, translating it to fiction in the process. On this visit and later ones—he was in Brighton again in 1841 after the birth of his son, Walter Savage Landor—he built up his knowledge of the town, which he was later to use in *Dombey and Son*. In that novel, the doctors recommend sea air for Paul Dombey, which Mrs Chick appears to support: 'a short absence from this house, the air of Brighton, and the bodily and mental training of as judicious a person as Mrs Pipchin for instance ...'[16] She leaves the rest unsaid, leaving Mr Dombey to assume that the sea air at Brighton will benefit Paul's health.

On his return from Brighton, Dickens sat for his portrait by Samuel Lawrence, which the artist presented to him. Dickens was so pleased with it that he asked Lawrence to paint a portrait of Kate.[17] The family remained at home in Doughty Street during most of the winter, but early in the New Year Dickens was off again, this time to the North to acquire first-hand information about 'the cheap schools of Yorkshire', which he had determined to expose in his next novel. He set off on 30 January from the 'Saracen's Head', London, with Browne, his illustrator, in severe wintry conditions. The experiences he gathered on the journey were vividly transferred to a similar coach journey taken by Nicholas, Squeers and the unfortunate boys destined for Dotheboys Hall.

> The night and the snow came on together, and dismal enough they were. There was no sound to be heard but the howling of the wind; for the noise of the wheels, and the tread of the horses' feet were rendered inaudible by the thick coating of snow which covered the ground, and was fast increasing every moment.[18]

Soon after this the coach overturns, but nothing so alarming happened to Dickens:

> At eleven we reached a bare place with a house standing alone in the midst of a dreary moor, which the guard informed us was Greta Bridge. I was in a perfect agony of apprehension, for it was fearfully cold, and there were no outward signs of anybody being up in the house. But to our great joy we discovered a comfortable room, with drawn curtains and a most blazing fire. In half an hour they gave us a smoking supper and a bottle of mulled port (in which we drank your health), and then we retired to a couple of capital bedrooms, in each of which there was a rousing fire half-way up the chimney.[19]

This was the George and New Inn at Greta Bridge.

Next morning they enjoyed an enormous breakfast (described in Chapter 10, page 120)—a meal which later inspired the one ordered by John Browdie on his honeymoon in London:

> ... the usual furniture of a tea-table was displayed in neat and inviting order, flanked by large joints of roast and boiled, a tongue, a pigeon pie, a cold fowl, a tankard of ale and other little matters of the like kind, which, in degenerate towns and cities are generally understood to belong

more particularly to solid lunches, stage-coach dinners, or unusually substantial breakfasts.[20]

Dickens's next letter to Forster describes his meeting with the Yorkshireman at Barnard's Castle, an incident he used in his Preface to the first 'cheap edition' of *Nickleby* (see also Chapter 10).

Waiting at Darlington for a coach to take them to York, Dickens was very annoyed to read what was called *A Brief Autobiography of Boz*, in a copy of *The Durham Advertiser*, written by an Irish journalist, Dr Mackenzie, who was to write a life of Dickens in 1870. The 'autobiography' was full of inaccuracies regarding the money earned by Dickens for writing *Pickwick* and editing *Bentley's Miscellany*. Dickens wrote an indignant letter to the newspaper denying these statements, which began 'Dr Mackenzie, whoever he may be, knows as much of me as of the meaning of the word autobiography . . .'[21]

Before returning to London, Dickens and Browne attended services in York Minster and saw the famous Five Sisters window. They stayed at the Black Swan Hotel. Dickens, on his return to Doughty Street, made a start on the writing of his third book, *Nicholas Nickleby*.

Wishing to be out of town when the first number appeared, Dickens took Kate, who was ill, to stay at the Star and Garter Hotel, Richmond. If his wife had not improved in health, Dickens planned to take her to Brighton again. However, she recovered enough to enjoy the celebration dinner with Forster.

By June 1838 Dickens was staying at Twickenham Park, or as he termed it in one of his letters, 'Gammon Lodge'. This was 4 Ailsa Park Villas, or Down House, Isleworth Road, Twickenham. It still stands, near the Southern Railway's St Margaret's Station, and is to be preserved. When staying here, for part of the summer, Dickens ran a Balloon Club for the children, though he brought the grown-ups into it as well. He wrote to Forster:

I am requested to inform you, that at a numerous meeting of the Gammon Aeronautical Association for the Encouragement of Science and the Consumption of Spirits (of Wine)—Thomas Beard Esquire, Mrs Charles Dickens, Charles Dickens Esquire, the Snodgering Blee,

Popem Jee, and other distinguished characters being present and assenting, the vote of censure of which I enclose a copy was unanimously passed upon you for gross negligence in discharge of your duty and most unjustifiable disregard of the best interests of the Society.[22]

Snodgering Blee and Popem Jee were the first of many nicknames bestowed upon the children, these two referring to Charles and Mamie. Mamie was also called Mild Glo'ster and later Katie became Lucifer Box, both expressive of their natures. The most fantastic of all the nicknames was possibly that bestowed upon the last son, Edward Bulwer Lytton—Plornishmaroontigoonter, later shortened to Plorn.

Forster was appointed President of the Balloon Club on condition that he supplied the balloons. Beard was the Honorary Secretary. It seems that weather presented the same problem in those days as it does now, for in a letter to Miss Agnes Strickland, the historian, Dickens remarks upon the phenomenon of a day of sunshine which decoyed him suddenly away, since which surprising appearance he had been looking out patiently for another.[23] Whilst at Twickenham, Dickens visited Eel Pie Island, a great attraction at that time; he later introduced it into *Nicholas Nickleby*, in which Miss Morleena Kenwigs receives an invitation to repair per steamer from Westminster Bridge unto Eel Pie Island at Twickenham, there to make merry upon a cold collation, bottled beer, shrub and shrimps, and to dance in the open air.[24]

On 28 June 1838, the Dickens family came to town to see the coronation of Queen Victoria. For this purpose Dickens took a room on the third floor of a house on the route of the procession. The next day he had to write to the proprietor asking for the return of a picnic basket they had left behind. He also wrote to Forster about his contribution to an article about the coronation, due to appear in *The Examiner*.

Early in July, Bentley had been invited to join Dickens on a visit to Hampton Court, and it was suggested he should take a boat from Hungerford Market. Steamers left from the north end of Hungerford Bridge for Hampton Court.[25]

Early in September 1838 Dickens and Kate spent a short holiday in the Isle of Wight, first staying at John Groves' Needles Hotel, Alum Bay, and then moving on to Ventnor.

It would be some eleven years before he returned, to Bonchurch, near Ventnor, for a holiday, only to find that the climate of the island did not agree with him. It was during the summer of 1838 that he first turned his thoughts to a possible visit to America, which was to be an accomplished fact four years later.[26]

On 29 October 1838, Dickens and Browne left for a tour of the Midlands and North Wales, partly to obtain background for future books. Dickens desired to see the cotton mills and the working conditions in the industrial areas. It was constantly in his mind to 'strike the heaviest blow in my power' for the workers in these mills, but he was not to do so until *Hard Times*, written in 1854.

The pair left from the coach office near Hungerford Market and enjoyed a very cold but pleasant ride to Leamington, where they stopped at what Dickens termed 'an excellent Inn—Copps's Hotel'. From here they went to Kenilworth, which he found 'delightful—beautiful beyond expression', and noted it as a very desirable summer resort, where he could lie about among the ruins reading a book. Warwick Castle yielded 'fine Pictures', and then on to Stratford, where he merely noted in his diary 'visitors—scribblers—and an old woman', doubting whether the latter knew about Shakespeare.[27] Possibly she was a guide or curator, but neither the diary nor the letters clarify her identity.

From here, Dickens and Browne went to Birmingham and finally to the White Lion at Shrewsbury. From here, on 1 November, Dickens wrote to Kate, who had written to him at that address:

> I received your welcome letter on arriving here last night, and am rejoiced to hear that the dear children are so much better. I hope that in your next or your next but one I shall learn that they are quite well. A thousand kisses to them—I wish I could convey them myself.[28]

He refers to the hotel at Leamington where they found a 'roaring fire, an elegant dinner, a snug room and capital beds all ready'. Kenilworth, Warwick Castle and Stratford are all mentioned, and this part of the country was to be recalled later in *Dombey and Son*, when Mr Dombey meets his second wife Edith and they tour the sights. Dickens's father had presumably recommended him to travel to Shrewsbury via Bridgnorth, but this he found impracticable for there were no coaches. They were obliged to travel via Birmingham and Wolverhampton 'through miles of cinder-paths and blazing furnaces and roaring steam engines and such a mass of dirt gloom and misery as I never before witnessed'.[29] All this was later to be recalled in his next book, *The Old Curiosity Shop*, when Nell and her Grandfather wander on foot through the Black Country. Compare his vivid word pictures in *The Old Curiosity Shop* with the words of his letter to Kate:

> A long suburb of red-brick houses,—some with patches of garden ground, where coal dust and factory smoke darkened the shrinking leaves and coarse rank flowers, and where the struggling vegetation sickened and sank under the hot breath of kiln and furnace ... on every side, and far as the eye could see into the heavy distance, tall chimneys, crowding on each other, and presenting that endless repetition of the same dull, ugly, form, which is the horror of oppressive dreams, poured out their plague of smoke, obscured the light, and made foul the melancholy air. On mounds of ashes by the wayside, sheltered only by a few rough boards, or rotten pent house roofs, strange engines spun and writhed like tortured creatures; clanking their iron chains, shrieking in their rapid whirl from time to time as though in torment unendurable, and making the ground tremble with their agonies.
>
> Or at night:
> ... night in this dreadful spot!—night, when the smoke was changed to fire; when every chimney spirited up its flame, and places, that had been dark vaults all day, now shone red-hot ...[30]

Although this was a kind of holiday, Dickens was 'photographing' these pictures in his mind for future use. The journalist was still very much in evidence within the novelist. At Stratford, he mentioned that he was very ill with a pain in his side (his old trouble from his younger days) and was obliged to take henbane to get some sleep. From here the tour continued to Llangollen through mountains, past aqueducts, to an old abbey, Valle Crucis, at the top of a mountain, staying at the Hand Hotel, which they found good.[31] Then on to Bangor, Capel Curig, Conway, Chester, Birkenhead, and finally to the Adelphi Hotel at Liverpool, where they met Forster, who had been advised to travel by train—on the Grand Junction railway from Birkenhead to

Liverpool. With Forster they went to Manchester. The
London to Birmingham railway had been opened the
previous September, and Dickens travelled back on it to
Euston, on 7 November.

It was at a dinner during this visit to Manchester that
Dickens with Forster and Browne met Daniel and William
Grant, who were later introduced into *Nicholas Nickleby* as
the Cheeryble Brothers. Dickens was again in Manchester
in January 1839, on a flying visit. During these visits he saw
what he called the worst cotton mill and the best, but found
no great difference between them.

Before long, his father's financial troubles reached a
climax, or at least came to his notice, and he was perforce
obliged to go off to Devonshire to find his parents somewhere to live, where they might be out of temptation (see
Chapters 6 and 7). Letters to his wife, Forster and Mitton
describe his activities in Alphington.

Early in May, Dickens could at last contemplate a
holiday, having, as he hoped, settled his father's affairs, and
went to stay with his family at Elm Cottage, Petersham.
Beresford Chancellor, in his *History of Richmond and
District*, quoting from a note contained in a parish magazine,
said that Dickens also occupied Woodbine Cottage, which
stands in part of the grounds adjoining Elm Cottage (now
Elm Lodge). There are no letters extant from the Woodbine
Cottage address to substantiate this, though there are some
headed 'Petersham'. Dickens's previous brief visit to
Petersham had been in August and September 1836, and
it is possible that he may have been in Woodbine Cottage
then. The only detail he gave of the address at that time was
Mrs Denman's, Petersham, Near Richmond.

From Elm Cottage Dickens wrote to Forster about a
visit to London to see Macready in one of his favourite
parts in *Virginius*.[32] He was still working on *Nickleby*,
writing to Charles Hicks about corrections in the proofs.[33]

In June, Dickens was attending the rehearsals of *Henry V*,
Macready's production at Covent Garden.[34] Having
arranged in March to sit for William Behnes, a sculptor,
Dickens notified him in his own facetious manner that he
had moved out of town:

Left his home
On the evening of Tuesday the Thirteenth of April last
A Remarkable Dog
answering to the name of Boz.
He had on at the time a white collar marked with the initials
C D (in marking ink) and was last seen, in company with
some other dogs, lying on the banks of the Thames at
Richmond.
He is undoubtedly a Setter,
And the property of Mr Behnes of Osnaburgh Street,
Regent's Park.
He has been traced to
Elm Cottage, Petersham, Surrey
where it appears probable he will remain until the end of the
summer.[35]

The letter continues in this vein with an invitation to the
sculptor to go down to Petersham for dinner.

While at Petersham, Dickens received pressing invitations
to dine with the Berry sisters, two friends of Horace
Walpole, who collected celebrities at their house in Petersham. Dickens had to refuse the first invitation, but later
acceded to their request to meet him.[36] They both lie
buried in the little churchyard of the ancient church at
Petersham. Dickens no doubt suffered during his career
from such people, and made fun of them even before the
Berry sisters' approach through the character Mrs Leo
Hunter (the literary lion hunter).

Both Beard and Maclise, among many others, were
invited to stay at Petersham. To Maclise, who had been ill,
Dickens wrote:

> Come down—Come down—Revive yourself by country air—Come
> down—and that without loss of time—and leave the rest to me, and
> I'll warrant you good health for 12 months at least . . . Beard is hearty,
> new and thicker ropes have been put up at the tree, the little birds have
> flown, their very nests have disappeared, the roads about are jewelled
> after dusk by glow worms, the leaves are all out and the flowers too,
> swimming feats from Petersham to Rickmond Bridge have been achieved
> before breakfast, I myself have risen at 6 and plunged head foremost
> into the water to the astonishment and admiration of all beholders.[37]

The house at Petersham still remains, as Elm Lodge.

Part of the large grounds have been sold for building purposes, but there is still quite an extensive garden left, in which Dickens and his family once played. The garden contains an exceptionally tall and straight oak tree, which must have been a young sapling when Dickens was there, and also an arboreal curiosity nicknamed an 'oakacia', an acacia in which an oak tree is growing—planted no doubt by a squirrel.

To Laman Blanchard, the Philadelphian publisher, Dickens refers in a letter to Petersham as '. . . these remote and distant parts, with the chain of mountains formed by Richmond Hill, presenting an almost insurmountable barrier between me and the busy world'.[38] He arranged to meet Blanchard at the Covent Garden Theatre.

In a long letter to Forster written from Petersham, Dickens set out his ideas for a future business association with the publishers Chapman and Hall, with whom he wished to remain because of their fair treatment. He also detailed his project for a new literary venture. This was to be a weekly magazine on the lines of *The Tatler*, *The Spectator* and *Goldsmith's Bee*. It was to contain articles on various subjects, some written by other contributors. He proposed re-introducing Mr Pickwick and Sam Weller, also the figures of Gog and Magog, all providing stories in a little club or knot of characters. A certain number of weekly publications would constitute a volume, to be published at regular intervals. In other words, Dickens wanted to move away from the twenty-part monthly serial story, which he thought might become wearisome to his readers. Dickens proposed that he should have full editorial control of the new magazine and a substantial share in the profits. Forster was to negotiate with the publishers; by that time, he had become Dickens's business manager and adviser.[39]

Dickens also submitted these proposals to Thomas Mitton for his comments and legal opinion.[40] The eventual result was *Master Humphrey's Clock*, but public demand soon obliged Dickens to revert to long stories, which although created for the framework of *Master Humphrey* were later to become separate publications, *The Old Curiosity Shop* and *Barnaby Rudge*. The latter was the story he had been planning five years previously, originally for Macrone.

In the meantime, Dickens continued to issue invitations to numerous friends to stay at Petersham. It seemed that Dickens was forever anxious to fill the house with company. Invitations went out to Maclise,[41] Angus Fletcher,[42] Mitton[43] (who had been ill) and Macready,[44] among others. To Fletcher, who was occupied in making a bust of the novelist, Dickens threatened that if his invitation to Petersham was not accepted, he would 'wear an entirely new face' whenever he went out and hence disgrace the bust. This marble bust is now in the Dickens House Museum, and is reckoned to be a good likeness of Dickens's appearance whilst at Doughty Street.

Dickens at last found it possible to accept Miss Burdett Coutts's invitation to dine with her. He had also been corresponding with a Miss Sarah Austin, a writer and educationalist who, after reading the last number of *Nickleby*, was anxious to meet the author. He was obliged to postpone his meeting with her, however, and also to decline an invitation from Lady Holland, owing to a prior engagement to be godfather at the christening of Macready's son, Henry.

The Petersham district was introduced into the story of Nickleby, part of which he wrote there. Not far from Elm Cottage is the entrance to the historic Ham House, through a gateway and along an imposing avenue of beautiful old elm trees which Dickens describes on the occasion of the duel between Sir Mulberry Hawk and Lord Verisopht:

> They stopped at the avenue gate and alighted ... all four walked in profound silence up the aisle of stately elm trees, which meeting far above their heads, formed a long green perspective of gothic arches, terminating, like some old ruin in the open sky ... at length they turned to the right and came into some fields beyond.[45]

Here the duel is fought and Lord Verisopht killed.

Many times I have taken Dickens enthusiasts along that stately avenue, into the fields beside the river in one of which the duel was fought. Alas, the stately elms had to be sacrificed when they became unsafe, and a new avenue planted some years ago is slowly growing up, but it will be many years, if ever, before the trees become interlaced above one's head again. The walk can still be taken, however, and in those riverside fields one can recall the close of that tragic chapter:

> So died Lord Verisopht, by the hand which he had loaded with gifts . . . The sun came proudly up in all his majesty, the noble river ran its winding course, the leaves quivered and rustled in the air, the birds poured their cheerful songs from every tree, the short-lived butterfly fluttered its little wings; and all the light of life and day came on, and amidst it all, and pressing down the grass whose every blade bore twenty tiny leaves, lay the dead man, with his stark and rigid face turned upwards to the sky.[46]

What a fine melodramatic picture Dickens conjured out of his wanderings in those lovely surroundings.

The Dickenses' next visit to Broadstairs was two years after their first one, this time for a month. On this occasion they took a complete house—no more humble High Street lodgings. To Forster Dickens wrote: 'There were no lodgings at Ramsgate (thank Heaven!) and after spending a night at the Hotel there,' (according to his diary, this was the Royal Hotel) 'we came on here, and with great difficulty established ourselves for a month—we couldn't get it for a shorter term.' The house was 40 Albion Street, which Dickens described as being:

> two doors from the Albion Hotel where we had that merry night two years ago, and has the most beautiful view of the sea from its bay-windows that you can imagine. It is a *house*—not a lodging—has a comfortable sitting-room with the view aforesaid, a large bedroom with ditto, a ditto nursery with ditto—kitchens et cetera in the usual places, entrances front and back, surprisingly clean beds, and a costively inconvenient water-closet.[47]

The rent was £21 a month.

This house later became part of the Royal Albion Hotel, and when some years later Dickens stayed at the hotel he was pleased to find that he was occupying his old premises. Visitors staying at the Royal Albion now who visit its little bar are actually in Dickens's original sitting-room. He stayed here in the hotel in 1859 and on that occasion wrote to Mamie and Katie his daughters:

> I have been moved here, and am now, (Ballard having added to the

hotel a house we lived in three years), in our old dining-room and sitting-room, and our old drawing-room is a bedroom.[48]

A year later, Mrs Dickens suffered a very alarming experience whilst staying at Broadstairs. Dickens was returning from town one day in August after bringing his boys up to school, and had arranged that Kate should meet him at Margate. As she was not at the agreed meeting-place, he walked along the road in the direction from which she should have come and met her, in a two-horse carriage, with the youth who had been driving her in their small chaise bruised and bandaged on the box behind. In his letter to Forster, Dickens said:

> You may faintly imagine my amazement at encountering this carriage ... At the top of a steep hill on the road, with a ditch on each side the pony bolted, whereupon what does John do but jump out! He says he was thrown out, but it cannot be. The reins immediately became entangled in the wheels, and away went the pony down the hill madly, with Kate inside rending the Isle of Thanet with her screams. The accident might have been a fearful one, if the pony had not, thank Heaven, on getting to the bottom, pitched over the side; breaking the shaft and cutting her hind legs, but in the most extraordinary manner smashing her own way apart. She tumbled down, a bundle of legs with her head tucked underneath, and left the chaise standing on the bank! A Captain Devaynes and his wife were passing in their carriage at the moment, saw the accident with no power of preventing it, got Kate out, laid her on the grass, and behaved with infinite kindness. All's well that ends well, and I think she's really none the worse for the fright. John is in bed a good deal bruised, but without any broken bone, and likely soon to come right; though for the present plastered all over, and, like Squeers, a brown paper parcel chock-full of nothing but groans ...[49]

Updown House, where Captain Devaynes and his wife lived, still stands, near the hill where the accident apparently happened.

Near the Royal Albion Hotel stands the original of Betsey Trotwood's cottage. Here in Dickens's time lived a woman named Mary Pearson Strong who would not allow anyone to ride a donkey across the cliff top in front of her cottage. Dickens was so amused that he put her into *David Copperfield* as Betsey Trotwood, and to save her embarrassment said that the cottage was at Dover. In recent years this cottage has been bequeathed to the local council, thanks to its last owners, Miss Dora Tattam and Miss Gladys Waterer. Here an excellent little museum has been established, and Betsey's parlour recreated.

At one end of the bay stands Bleak House, in which Dickens spent holidays some time after leaving Doughty Street. In his time it was called Fort House, and although he may have planned the story of *Bleak House* when staying there, he neither wrote it there nor looked upon this building as being the Bleak House of the novel, which he said was at St Albans. The building has been extended but the original part occupied by Dickens is now a museum. He did, however, write parts of *David Copperfield* here. A costume garden party is held in its grounds during the annual Dickens Festival held in Broadstairs in June, which is attended by people from all over the world. At those times one can see Mr Pickwick strolling along the front, obviously avoiding the widows, but with a weather eye open for all the young girls, or Bill Sikes beating poor Nancy through the town, or Mr Dick trying to fly his kite, and many great characters written about by Dickens whilst he lived in this little seaside resort.

Some of Dickens's friends came down by boat from London Bridge, as he often did himself. Whilst living in the house in Albion Street he sent up to Doughty Street for their own cook, for apparently a local woman recommended as a temporary by their landlady had got drunk, lain down in front of the house and addressed the passers-by for some hours. Dickens invited Forster to come down and stay with them, which he did for a few days:

> Take the *Ramsgate* boat from London Bridge at 9 precisely. Say when you draw near here, that you are for Broadstairs, and come ashore in the boat which will come along-side for you. If the weather should be so rough that the boat can't come off (not probable), go on to Ramsgate and return—2 miles—by fly.[50]

Angus Fletcher, the sculptor, was invited five days later to occupy the spare bed. Dickens had evidently been asking Fred, his brother, about two plaster figures in Doughty Street which he wanted for the dining-room at Broadstairs. They were called Night and Morning after Thorwaldson, the Scandinavian sculptor. These two statuettes, listed in the drawing-room section of the sales catalogue for Gad's Hill, were sold after Dickens's death.[51]

By 18 September 1839, Dickens was writing to Forster that he would have to come to town that weekend to save delaying the proofs of *Nickleby*. He goes on to describe a storm they had been having:

> It has been blowing great guns here for the last three days, and last night—I wish you could have seen it—there was *such* a sea! Fred (who is here) and I, staggered down to the pier and creeping under the lee of a large boat which was high and dry, watched it breaking for nearly an hour. Of course we came back wet through, but it was most superb. One steamboat after getting to Ramsgate could not make her way into the harbour and was obliged to go back to Margate and put in there, and the boat from London didn't come at all. Heaven knows what became of it—nobody here does.[52]

It was a later storm, witnessed at Broadstairs, that Dickens used for the famous chapter of *David Copperfield* containing the account of the tempest at Yarmouth, in which Ham and Steerforth are drowned.

He also made fun of Cruikshank's illustration for Ainsworth's serial of *Jack Sheppard*, in *Bentley's Miscellany*, called 'Jonathen Wild throwing Sir Rowland down the well-hole'. Dickens wrote:

> A famous subject for an illustration by George—Jonathen Wild forcing Mrs Sheppard down the grown-up seat of a gloomy privy, and Blueskin (Sheppard's partner) or any such second robber cramming a child (anybody's child) down the little hole.[53]

(This was when the toilets often included several sizes of seats to accommodate adults and children.)

His next batch of letters from Broadstairs from 21 September onwards were invitations to the *Nickleby* celebration dinner on 5 October. He also wrote to Thomas Ellar, a pantomime dancer who played Harlequin to Grimaldi's clown. Ellar, having read Grimaldi's *Memoirs*, wanted Dickens to edit his memoirs as well. This Dickens declined to do.[54] He was back in Doughty Street by the beginning of October.

After moving from Doughty Street, Dickens paid quite regular visits to Broadstairs for many years. He loved the little semi-circular bay and occupied a number of houses there, most of which have since been marked with tablets to that effect. Indeed, so many have been marked in this way that one house-owner with an ancient cottage has put up a tablet on its wall saying 'Dickens did NOT live here'.

CHAPTER 12

'These garish lights'

'THESE garish lights' he called them, and so they were in those days—a row of smoky oil and later flaring gas lamps—naked flames, incredibly dangerous and both equally hot, melting the greasepaint of the actors and actresses behind them. That row of lights divided two worlds: the world behind, mysterious and glamorous, and make-believe; the world in front, credulous and happy to accept the make-believe. The life of the actor was a closed book to the ordinary audience; if the stage effects went wrong, they were accepted for what they were meant to be. Now, unfortunately, thanks in great measure to the prying press, the mechanics of every stage effect are dragged into the daylight and the private lives of stage performers made public—more's the pity. Gone is the real glamour of the theatre: the one endeavour now seems to be to present life itself, and often the sordid and unpleasant side of it at that.

Dickens loved to anticipate the excitement waiting behind 'the curtain that hid such gorgeous mysteries . . . what a glow was that, which burst upon them all, when that long, clear, brilliant row of lights came slowly up . . .'[1] He was to write that only a short time after leaving Doughty Street.

First, then, came his boyhood days, when he no doubt enjoyed being exhibited by his father, singing comic songs and duets with his sister. Then in his brief schooldays, his presentation of the toy theatre. Later, in his teens, he wrote and presented plays at home for a select few, including an unsuccessful attempt to 'show off' before a girl (Maria Beadnell) he madly loved. In his early days at work his love of the theatre showed itself through his constant visits to it, often to the half-price theatre (referred to in 'Making a Night of it', from *Sketches by Boz*, and elsewhere).

At twenty, his desire to go on the stage was frustrated when a severe cold in the face prevented him from attending an audition. When he was older, his writing kept him too busy to be involved with the theatre. In larger and more adaptable houses than Doughty Street, he was later to present plays for his children at Christmas, then plays for himself and his friends, even to the climax of playing before his Queen in 1857 when he was forty-five; these performances were followed by successful amateur dramatic tours in aid of charity. Finally he began to give readings of his works, first for charity then professionally—illuminated by those garish lights.

His attempts at writing for the theatre were perhaps the least successful of his literary endeavours. They date mostly from the time just prior to his coming to Doughty Street. In December 1835, Dickens was writing to J. P. Hullah, composer and teacher of choral music, suggesting that an idea for an operetta with a Venetian setting they had evidently been discussing should be dropped in favour of one with an English theme.[2] Dickens at that time knew little or nothing about Venetian or Italian backgrounds for plots.

By May the following year some of the music had been written, and Dickens was contacting various music publishers to see if they were interested in taking on the project, among them Cramer's of Regent Street, Coventry and Hollier of 71 Dean Street, Soho, and Goulding and D'Almaine of 20 Soho Square. Dickens suggested that it would be best for Hullah, the musical member of the partnership, to treat with them.[3] Between writing sketches for his newspaper, writing *Pickwick*, covering elections at Ipswich for his newspaper and courting Catherine, Dickens was completing the words of the operetta, and in July was inviting Mr and Mrs Macrone to join him with other friends to hear it run through.[4] But in August Dickens was still impatiently waiting for the completion of the music: 'When, oh *when* will this Music be ready?'[5] Some of it, however, was being tried a week or so later, and Braham, the owner of St James's Theatre, was very satisfied with it—also G. F. Stansbury, the musical director and conductor of the theatre.[6]

A few days later, Dickens was offered £30 for a farce in

two acts to be called *The Strange Gentleman*, a stage adaptation of his story 'The Great Winglebury Duel' from *Sketches by Boz*. This was to be produced at St James's Theatre on 1 October, and it proved a very good vehicle for Harley, the comedian. T. F. Beale, a partner of Cramer & Co., who had purchased the music of *The Village Coquettes*, requested that a verse in one of the songs should be omitted or altered, because the young ladies in the chorus objected to singing the line 'Well warmed to bed we go'. Under protest, Dickens substituted an alternative line, but wrote to Hullah:

> If the young ladies are especially horrified at the bare notion of anybody's going to bed, I have no objection to substitute for the objectionable line—
>
> > 'Around old stories go'.
>
> But you may respectfully signify to Cramers that I will see them d---d before I make any further alteration ... I am sure on reflection you will see that we ought not to emasculate the very spirit of a song to suit boarding-schools ...[7]

By the new year, Dickens was referring to a little sketch he wrote long before he was Boz, called 'Cross Purposes', but it was later renamed *Is She His Wife? or Something Singular*, and Harley appeared in it in March 1837.[8] The two pieces, *The Strange Gentleman* and *Is She His Wife?*, wear very well even today, and are both effective and amusing when properly produced and presented. I recall with pleasure an excellent theatre-in-the-round production of the first-named at Portsmouth by the Arena Players, in 1970; and the second farce was very successfully revived at the 'Lamb and Flag', off Garrick Street, in 1971.[9]

The only other writing Dickens did for the theatre about this time was whilst he was at Doughty Street. He had a great ambition to write something for Macready to perform, and he completed a farce called *The Lamplighter*. In December 1838 Dickens read it to Macready who, although he thought the dialogue good and full of point, had doubts about the meagreness of the plot. Obviously not a suitable vehicle for Macready, *The Lamplighter* was eventually withdrawn by Dickens, apparently without any hurt feelings. Someone must have been very tactful! It is significant that Macready remarked on the theatrical ability of Dickens and noted in his diary that Dickens read as well as an experienced actor.[10]

Dickens then seems to have abandoned his ideas of writing for the theatre until much later—1867, when he collaborated with Wilkie Collins in adapting their joint Christmas story 'No Thoroughfare' into a drama, in which Fechter, the Swiss actor, appeared at the Lyceum; Dickens later gave advice for the Paris production of the play.

Soon after arriving at Doughty Street, Dickens was in frequent correspondence with Harley regarding a revival of *The Village Coquettes*, but by then, less than a year after its first performance, he did not seem very proud of his authorship of that work. Remarking on the altered book when it was in rehearsal,[11] he requested the omission of 'Boz' from the bills: 'After the choppings and changings which this most unfortunate piece has undergone, I am not anxious to remind the Public that I am the perpetrator.'[12] For this reason, if no other, it seems he would not easily have made a successful dramatist; he could not have accepted happily the lot of the unfortunate theatrical author who sees his work changed—indeed, mutilated—as it is being produced.

In the spring, Dickens still had in mind the possibility of writing a play: 'I have considered the terms on which I could afford just now to sell Mr Braham the acting copyright in London of an entirely new piece for the St James's Theatre; and I could not sit down to write one in a single act of about an hour long, under a hundred pounds. For a new piece in two acts, a hundred and fifty pounds . . .'[13] The price of Dickens's services was rising steeply.

In September 1839, Dickens pointed out in a letter the difficulties of writing for the theatre, and criticized a play written and sent to him by J. A. Overs, a London cabinet-maker, with whose literary efforts the novelist had helped:

> . . . of the play itself, I cannot speak favourably. The production is most honorable and creditable to you, but it would not benefit you, either in pocket or reputation, if it were printed,—and acted, I do not think it ever could be. Not to mention that the verse contains most singular instances of inverted expressions (which I may describe more familiarly as putting the cart before the horse) and many words not to be found in the language—not to mention these faults which are easily susceptible of correction, there are some in the plot and characters,

which seem to me incurable. The father is such a dolt, and the villain *such* a villain, the girl so especially credulous and the means used to deceive them so very slight and transparent, that the reader *cannot* sympathise with their distresses. Action too is terribly wanting, and the characters not being strongly marked (except in improbabilities) the dialogues grow tedious and wearisome. I read it with great care, and not long ago either, but I don't remember at this moment any difference in the mode or matter of their speech which enables me to distinguish, in recollection, one character from the other—except the maiden lady and the villain, of whom the former is very good, and the latter but an average villain who speaks in dashes and interjections and constantly interrupts himself . . .

I firmly believe that if this play had been written by Sheridan Knowles or Sir Edward Bulwer, it would not have been acted . . . Remember how very difficult it is to produce a good play, how very few men can do it, and how many fail and how few try or if they do try, ever permit their trials to see the light.[14]

From Mary Hogarth's death until about the end of 1837, Dickens seemed to have been avoiding St James's Theatre. He was probably thinking of the night he was there with her, when he wrote to Harley:

As I do not know where to find Mrs Braham now . . . may I rely on you to ask her to leave word with the man at the door to let us have a pit or proscenium box *on the same side as that on which we used to sit; but not a box on the same tier, or opposite.* Old recollections make us shun our old haunts, or the sight of them.[15]

Mrs Braham managed St James's Theatre.[16]

Dickens had visited other theatres in the meantime, but perhaps not to the same extent as before. In September he shared a private box with Procter (Barry Cornwall) and Forster to see Macready as Leontes in *A Winter's Tale*, and invited Ainsworth to join them.[17] Whenever Dickens went away, he invariably made a point of attending the local theatre and at Brighton, in November, he saw Charles Kean in *The Honey Moon*.[18] Dickens was not very impressed with his acting.

Forster was dramatic critic for *The Examiner*, and in December Dickens sent him 'a good whack of copy' concerning 'Common Garden, the Delphi, and Saint James's'. He could not find time, he wrote, 'to do Doory Lane'. The plays on which he apparently reported were *Joan of Arc*, the

Maid of Orleans at Covent Garden, *Valsha* at the Adelphi, and *The Cabinet* at St James's.[19]

The same month he wrote to Yates, the producer and actor, at the Adelphi, asking if he could spare his private box to enable Mrs Dickens to see *Valsha*. The other boxes, he pointed out, were so closely packed that Kate, being in delicate health, was afraid. Dickens himself had braved the heat to review the play for Forster[20] (the heat in the theatres, particularly higher up, was very great in the days of oil and gas lamps), and thought Kate would enjoy it. He referred to it as 'a bad play but a gorgeous spectacle, most admirably got up'.

Again and again in his letters he refers to theatre-going, certainly his favourite relaxation from his close work at his desk. He told Forster early in 1838 that he had seen Talfourd's play, *The Athenian Captive*, at the Haymarket, in which Macready played Thoas, and considered it admirable.[21]

He not only supported the theatre most enthusiastically with his presence, but also financially, and whilst he was at Doughty Street, made frequent contributions to theatrical bodies, to which his bank book bears witness:

28 Mar 1837	Theatrical Fund	£5. 5. 0.
26 Oct 1839	„ „	5. 0. 0.
25 Mar 1839	Artists' Benevolent Fund	5. 0. 0.
16 Apr „	„ „ „ „	7. 12. 0.
28 May „	„ „ „ „	9. 9. 0.
1 Mar „	Drury Lane Theatre Fund	5. 0. 0.

In March he was writing to Macready:

Have you any objection to allow my name to be put down among the admissable at the Stage Door? I have passed (I don't know by what authority, now I come to think of it) fifty times this season, but as the porter was not particularly sober last night, and exceedingly insolent, I should like to have right upon my side—having which, I can spare the civility.[22]

He also referred in this letter to a good notice of Macready's performance in *Coriolanus*. On display in the Dickens House Museum is one of Dickens's theatre passes—a small ivorine pendant, admitting him to Her Majesty's Theatre.

His two chief contacts in the theatre were Macready and
Harley, representing, as it were, drama and comedy. In the
summer of 1838, Harley was being offered 'a small box
with a spare bed in it' for Sunday night at Twickenham
Park.[23] Occasionally his writing of the *Oliver* and *Nickleby*
instalments prevented Dickens from going to the play, even
though *Hamlet* or *Othello* were on the bill at Covent Garden
Theatre.[24] By the end of October 1838, however, *Oliver
Twist* was completed, as Macready recorded in his diary
that Dickens had made use of his box. Towards the end of
the year he was back at St James's Theatre, promising to see
Harley there;[25] or asking the actor to come after dinner to
Doughty Street, for his birthday, when the play in which he
was appearing was finished.[26] (Harley was playing Trinculo
in *The Tempest*.)

Even when away, Dickens attended the bespeak at
Shrewsbury, which reminded him of Miss Snevellicci's
benefit in *Nickleby*.[27] Back in town, if the writing of *Nickleby*
was advanced enough, he contemplated yet another visit to
the Adelphi.[28] In the New Year he refers to a Command
Performance at Covent Garden Theatre, the date of which
has been announced at very short notice.[29]

In Exeter he did *not* go to the theatre when Charles Kean
was playing Sir Giles Overreach. Dickens thought he might
upset himself by going, so he stayed away and read a book.
The play was Philip Massinger's *A New Way to Pay Old
Debts*. Dickens was rather sore on that subject, being down
in Devonshire to instal his parents in a cottage after settling
his father's debts.[30] He also referred to his absence from the
theatre in his letter to Kate.[31]

Later in the year came the news of Macready's retirement
from the management of Covent Garden Theatre; Dickens
wrote to him:

> I ought not to be sorry to hear of your abdication, but I am, notwith-
> standing—most heartily and sincerely sorry, for my own sake, and the
> sake of thousands who may now go and whistle for a Theatre—at least,
> such a Theatre as you gave them. And I do now in my heart believe
> that for a long and dreary time that exquisite delight has passed away. If
> I may jest with my misfortunes, and quote the Portsmouth critic of
> Mr Crummles's company, I say that 'as an exquisite embodiment of
> the poet's visions and a realisation of human intellectuality gilding with

refulgent light our dreamy moments, and laying open a new and magic world before the mental eye, the drama is gone—perfectly gone.'[32]

Dickens was quoting Mr Curdle in *Nicholas Nickleby*.

He attended Macready's farewell performance from Petersham and, writing to Blanchard, said:

> I shall be in town and at the theatre on Tuesday night. You will be there too, no doubt? In the proscenium box on the Bow Street side I will hold further converse with you when the play is over . . . Therefore are we preparing crowns and wreaths here, to shower upon the stage when that sad curtain falls and kivers up Shakespeare for years to come. I try to make a joke of it, but upon my word, when the night comes I verily believe I shall cry.[33]

On several occasions Dickens gave Macready plays to read: in July 1839 a translation from German by a Scottish lady, and in December, according to Macready's diary, Dickens gave him a play called *Glencoe* to read.[34]

Dickens was naturally very interested in stage adaptations of his own stories, of which there were many. By mid-March 1838, he was in contact with Frederick Yates, the actor, proposing to write a dramatic version of *Oliver Twist* by the beginning of September, thereby beating the theatrical pirates. Dickens made the same proposal to Macready through Forster, but the actor decided that it was quite impracticable for this story to be presented on the stage. Nothing came of either proposal. To Yates he wrote:

> I don't see the possibility of any other house doing it before your next opening night. If they do, it must be done in a very extraordinary manner, as the story (unlike that of Pickwick) is an involved and complicated one. I am quite satisfied that no one can have heard what I mean to do with the different characters in the end, inasmuch as at present, I don't quite know, myself; so we are tolerably safe on that head. Anyway I am quite sure that your name as the Jew, and mine as the author, would knock any other attempts quite out of the field.[35]

How wrong Dickens was! The fact that other dramatists did not know the outcome of the story did not deter them in any way. Yates himself produced a version—not by Dickens —in February 1839, at the Adelphi, in which he played Fagin, and his wife took Nancy. Mrs Keely played Oliver. Before this, however, five other theatres had produced their own versions. The novel was only half written when a version appeared at St James's Theatre, possibly by Gilbert à Beckett, with Harley as Bumble and Madame Sala as Mrs Corney. The play was so badly reviewed that it was taken off almost immediately—possibly after only two nights. One review called it 'a very meagre and dull affair and the sooner taken from the bills the better', and another, 'a thing more unfit for any stage, except that of a Penny Theatre we never saw'.

At the Pavilion, Mile End Road, was presented another adaptation which only lasted a very short time, by C. Z. Barnett. The most successful production was a 'serio-comic-burletta' by George Almar, in three acts and thirty-one scenes, at the Surrey Theatre, which took the plot up to the death of Sikes; it ran from November 1838 to February 1839, and beyond. Oliver was played by a Master Owen, specially engaged for the part. Dickens did not approve of it: Forster says that he lay down on the floor of his box for the last part of the performance. Why he did not walk out is a puzzle. In spite of Dickens's opinion, this version reached America and was presented in New York.

Yet a fourth version, by Thomas Greenwood, was produced at Sadler's Wells with a female hero, and in regard to this one Dickens commented:

> I have never seen Mrs Honnor to the best of my recollection; but from the mere circumstance of her being a Mrs, I should say at once that she was 'a many sizes too large' for Oliver Twist. If it be played by a female, it should be a very sharp girl of thirteen or fourteen—not more, or the character would be an absurdity.[36]

Mrs Honnor did play Oliver Twist in the Sadler's Wells production on 3 December 1838, and her husband, who was joint manager of the theatre with Thomas Greenwood, author of the adaptation, played Fagin. A fifth production was Edward Stirling's, at the City of London Theatre, who had previously adapted and produced *The Pickwick Club*. All these were produced before Yates presented his version in February, 1839.[37]

Edward Stirling also dramatized *Nicholas Nickleby* as it was being written, and Dickens went to see it at the Adelphi in November 1838. Forster was reviewing for *The Examiner* the *Oliver Twist* production at the Surrey Theatre the same evening, and could not get to the Adelphi to review *Nickleby* until later. Dickens therefore provided him with details of the part of the play he missed. He praised the skilful management and dressing of the boys, and the capital manner and speech of Fanny Squeers; also the presentation of her card party in Squeers's parlour. Mrs Keeley played Smike and Dickens thought both her first appearance inside Dotheboys Hall and the rest of her performance excellent.[38] He disliked, however, the reference to robins in her lines, put in by Stirling, and was horrified when he heard her speak them at rehearsal.[39]

Writing to Yates after the Adelphi visit, Dickens said he would be glad of an opportunity to tell Mrs Keeley and O. Smith—an actor who had played several Dickens character parts—how very highly he appreciated their Smike and Newman Noggs, and added: 'I put you out of the question altogether, for that glorious Mantalini is beyond all praise.'[40] Crummles was of course not in the earlier adaptations, for Dickens had not yet introduced him into the story. However, many other versions of *Nicholas Nickleby* were produced.

In the novel, Dickens seized the opportunity to make his protest against these piratical adaptations. When Nicholas attends the farewell dinner to the Crummleses, before they depart for America, he says to the literary gentleman beside him:

> For instance, you take the uncompleted books of living authors, fresh from their hands ... cut, hack, and carve them to the powers and capabilities of your actors ... hastily and crudely vamp up ideas not yet worked out by their original projector, but which have doubtless cost him many thoughtful days ... all this without his permission and against his will. Now, show me the distinction between such pilfering as this, and picking a man's pocket in the street.[41]

It has been generally accepted that the originals of the Crummles family in *Nickleby* were the Davenports with their 'Infant Phenomenon' Jean, who at the age of nine played Richard III and Shylock at Richmond Theatre, in 1837. It has also been stated, but not substantiated, that Dickens appeared at this old theatre—not the present one, but the earlier building across the Green, in which Edmund Kean acted. It seems unlikely, however, in the light of the rapid development of his literary career at that time, though Dickens may have appeared in the private theatres run by the Davenports in London—the Westminster Subscription Theatre in Tothill Street, for example in 1832. It is doubtful whether this can ever be proved or disproved, but it is certain that Dickens knew the theatre well from both sides of the footlights, and used his knowledge when writing those unforgettable scenes in *Nickleby*, and his paper 'Private Theatres', published in the *Evening Chronicle* in 1835.

Some years later, he was to indulge in ambitious amateur theatricals for charity and finally to give readings, with his own curtains, proscenium and row of flaring gas lamps, the gas lamps which inspired his famous farewell words when he finally concluded his appearances before the public: 'From these garish lights I now vanish for evermore.'

AFTERWORD

Two more members were added to the Dickens family during their occupation of Doughty Street: Mamie in 1838 and Kate in 1839. The house was becoming crowded, and larger premises were needed in which Dickens could entertain and live up to his improved circumstances. So once more he went house-hunting, but with no lively companion like Mary to accompany him. Between bouts of writing another book, *Barnaby Rudge*, which was not published until some years later, he was looking at prospective houses with Kate. He wrote to Mrs Macready: 'I have seen an extremely pretty house in Kent Terrace, where you used to live.'[1] Later he wrote to Mitton that Macready had told him that when he lived in Kent Terrace (two doors from No. 10) 'the stench from the stable at certain periods of the wind was so great that he could scarcely breathe'.[2] This house was definitely unsuitable. To Forster he mentioned that house-hunting seriously interfered with the writing of *Barnaby*.[3]

Finally, Kate and Dickens found the house they wanted— 1 Devonshire Terrace, York Gate, Regents Park, and Dickens told Forster: 'A house of great promise (and great premium) "undeniable" situation, and excessive splendour, is in view. Mitton is in treaty, and I am in ecstatic restlessness.'[4] He consequently wrote to his landlord, E. W. Banks:

> I have a proposition to make to you relative to leaving your house, which, under the circumstances, I think it very probable may meet your views as well as mine by enabling you to make whatever repairs or alterations you may deem advisable before letting it again, without losing rent or time in the meanwhile. Some repairs I presume you will deem it necessary to make at once, with a view to obtaining a Tenant on good terms. The drains for instance have been a serious annoyance to us, and although we have had plumbers in the house half a dozen times, we have not been able to make them last our time without often receiving strong notice of their being in the neighbourhood.
>
> The proposition I have to make to you, is this:- I will give you up

possession at Christmas (paying the rent to March) if you will take the fixtures off my hands. I purchased them when I came in and have improved and added to them since, and as they stand—excellent blinds being fitted in every window, and many little conveniences here and there—they certainly improve the appearance of the house and give it an air of much greater comfort and accommodation. There is some pattern furniture, namely the drawing-room carpet, the fender and fire-irons, the curtains and fitted cornices, and the oil cloth in the passage—all in the best condition. These I wish to offer to you, too. If you feel inclined to take them *all*, I propose they should be valued by any respectable person—Mr Handyside for instance who valued for you before—and in consideration of your taking the whole, I would make an abatement in the price of fifteen per cent upon his valuation . . .[5]

This proposition was accepted by the landlord, and so Dickens moved into a much larger and more luxurious house, where he was finally to cement his claim to fame by writing such books as *The Old Curiosity Shop, Barnaby Rudge, Martin Chuzzlewit, Dombey and Son, David Copperfield* and the *Christmas Books,* including the most famous short story of all—*A Christmas Carol.* But it was in Doughty Street that this young man, with little literary experience behind him, forged his way ahead despite domestic difficulties and setbacks, by sheer determination and hard work, to become the greatest of all novelists and the creator of more immortal characters than any writer before or after him. If Doughty Street is haunted, it is haunted by these great figures of fiction who were created within its walls. It was here that Dickens wrote those early books that have survived the passing of time and stand on our bookshelves today, great classics of literature.

NOTES

NOTES

Key to abbreviations used in the notes below

P L   *The Letters of Charles Dickens* (Pilgrim Edition, The Clarendon Press), edited by Madeline House and Graham Storey.

N L   *The Letters of Charles Dickens* (Nonesuch Press), edited by Walter Dexter.

E J   *Charles Dickens: His Tragedy and Triumph* (Oxford University Press), by Edgar Johnson.

D H   Dickens House Museum at 48 Doughty Street, London WC1.

D   *The Dickensian*, published quarterly by The Dickens Fellowship.

F   *Life of Dickens* (1928) by John Forster, annotated by J. W. T. Ley.

S   *A Portrait of Dickens* (J. M. Dent & Sons, 1928), by Ralph Straus.

S B B   *Sketches by Boz.*

P P   *Pickwick Papers.*

O T   *Oliver Twist.*

N N   *Nicholas Nickleby.*

O C S   *The Old Curiosity Shop.*

B R   *Barnaby Rudge.*

M C   *Martin Chuzzlewit.*

D S   *Dombey and Son.*

D C   *David Copperfield.*

G E   *Great Expectations.*

E D   *The Mystery of Edwin Drood.*

U T   *The Uncommercial Traveller.*

C C   *A Christmas Carol.*

R P   *Reprinted Pieces.*

The Oxford Press Illustrated Edition of the novels is referred to except where otherwise stated.

Chapter 1   'Room to swing a cat'

1	D C	Ch 35		
2	P L Vol 1	p. 139	Miss C. Hogarth	10 Mar 1838
3	M C	Ch 45		
4	O C S	Ch 35		
5	E D	Ch 20		
6	Ibid	Ch 11		
7	D H		Mary Hogarth to Mary Scott Hogarth	15 May 1836

8	D H	Handisyde			Mar 1837
9	E J Vol 1	p. 188			
10	D H	Cruikshank			Feb 1837
11	P L Vol 1	p. 244 Note 6			
12	D H	Grissell, Peto & Gardner		9 Jan	1838
13	D H	Original lease and other documents			
14	S B B	'The Boarding House'			
15	Ibid	'Horatio Sparkins'			
16	U T	'Some Recollections of Mortality'			
17	Ibid				
18	O T	Ch 51			
19	Ibid	Ch 2			
20	P L Vol 1	341	Ainsworth	D H 11 Dec	1837
21	P P	Ch 5			
22	D H	*The Sun*		20 Oct	1838
23	Ibid	Dickens's bank books			
24	O C S	Ch 36			
25	P P	Ch 32			
26	N L Vol 1	145/6	Dickens's diary		
27	P L Vol 1	339	Note 2		
28	D C	Ch 43			
29	Ibid	Ch 34			
30	M C	Ch 46			
31	P L Vol 1	248	Beard	D H 12 Apr	1837
32	D H	Dickens's bank book			
33	Ibid				
34	Ibid				
35	D H	Family Bible			
36	Ibid	Dickens family tree			

Chapter 2 *'The dearest friend I ever had'*

1	O T	Ch 29			
2	P L Vol 1	259	Beard	D H 17 May	1837
3	Ibid	390	Forster	25 Mar	1838
4	P L Vol 1	268	Unknown	8 Jun	1837
5	Ibid	263	Richard Johns	31 May	1837
6	Ibid	257	G. Thomson	8 May	1837
7	O C S	Ch 71			
8	P L Vol 1	258	Edward Chapman	12 May	1837
9	G E	Ch 35			
10	F Bk 2	Ch 8 160	Note		
11	N L Vol 1	519	Mrs Hogarth	8 May	1843
12	Ibid	440	Forster	26 Apr	1842
13	Ibid	624	Forster	30 Sep	1844

14	P L Vol 1		268	Unknown			Jun	1837
15	P L Vol 2		408	Mrs Hogarth		24	Oct	1841
16	P L Vol 1		260	Ainsworth		17	May	1838
17	P L Vol 2		181/2	Forster		7	Jan	1841
18	O T	Ch 33						

Chapter 3   *Uneasy partnerships*

1	D	1936/7	5	Chapman and Hall to Dickens		12	Feb	1836
2	P L Vol 1		185	Beard	D H	28	Oct	1836
3	Ibid		150	Macrone		9	May	1836
4	Ibid		648	Bentley Agreement	D H	22	Aug	1836
5	Ibid		649/50	Bentley Agreement	D H	4	Nov	1836
6	Ibid		650/1	Bentley Agreement	D H	17	Mar	1837
7	Ibid		190/1	Easthope		5	Nov	1836
8	Ibid		196	Easthope		18	Nov	1836
9	Ibid		196			18	Nov	1836
10	Ibid		196/7			18	Nov	1836
11	Ibid		197			18	Nov	1836
12	*Speeches*	(K.J. Fielding)		Newspaper Press Fund		20	May	1865
13	N L Vol 1		726	Forster				1845
14	P L Vol 1		549/50	Mitton		13	May	1839

Chapter 4   *'The Burlington Street brigand'*

1	P L Vol 1	292	Forster		5	Aug	1837
2	Ibid	279	Note 2				
3	Ibid	307/8	Cruikshank		16	Sep	1837
4	Ibid	309	Cruikshank		16	Sep	1837
5	Ibid	308/9	Bentley		16	Sep	1837
6	Ibid	654	Bentley Agreement	D H	28	Sep	1837
7	Ibid	337	Bentley		5	Dec	1837
8	Ibid	339/40	Bentley		7	Dec	1837
9	Ibid	401/2	Bentley		31	May	1838
10	Ibid	493/4	Forster		21	Jan	1839
11	Ibid						
12	Ibid	666/80	Bentley Agreements		22	Sep	1838
				and	27	Feb	1839
13	Ibid	616/8	Smithson and Mitton		16	Dec	1839
14	P L Vol 1	619	Beard		17	Dec	1839
15	P L Vol 2	471/3	Bentley Agreement		2	Jul	1840

Chapter 5   *Dining at Doughty Street*

1 *What Shall We Have for Dinner?*   Mrs C. Dickens

2	*Movable Feasts*		Arnold Palmer				
3	P L Vol 1	246	Forster			7 Apr	1837
4	Ibid	248	Beard	D H	12 Apr	1837	
5	Ibid	618	Beard	D H	17 Dec	1839	
6	Ibid	7	Note 3				
7	N N	Ch 3					
8	D	1955	58/66	'Charles Dickens and the Ross Family', W. J. Carlton			
9	P P	Ch 6					
10	P L Vol 1	76	Beard	D H	14 Oct	1835	
	Ibid	80	Beard	D H	24 Oct	1835	
	Ibid	286	Beard	D H	21 Jul	1837	
11	Ibid	249	Bentley		20 Apr	1837	
12	Ibid	253	Bentley		28 Apr	1837	
13	Ibid	253	Note 2				
14	Ibid	261	Bentley		23 May	1837	
15	Ibid	275	Mrs G. Hogarth	D H	Jun	1837	
16	Ibid	134	Note 2				
17	Ibid	275	Ainsworth		21 Jun	1837	
18	Ibid	277	Forster		22 Jun	1837 and Note 5	
19	Ibid	278	Forster		27 Jun	1837	
20	*The Dickens Circle*, J. W. T. Ley						
21	P L Vol 1	317	Forster		Oct	1837	
22	*The Dickens Circle*, J. W. T. Ley						
23	P P	Ch 43					
24	P L Vol 1	282/3	Ainsworth		14 Jul	1837	
25	Ibid	279	Bentley		27 Jun	1837	
26	Ibid	279	Note 1				
27	Ibid	167	Note 1				
28	Ibid	343	Forster		Dec	1837	
29	Ibid	347	Forster		Dec	1837	
30	Ibid	348	Forster		Dec	1837	
31	Ibid	364	Forster		Jan	1838	
32	Ibid	440	Forster		Oct	1838	
33	Ibid	457	Forster		19 Nov	1838	
34	Ibid	510	Forster		Feb	1839	
35	Ibid	510/1	Forster		21 Feb	1839	
36	Ibid	513	Note 1				
37	Ibid	298	Forster		28 Aug	1837	
38	Ibid	160	Note 2				
39	Ibid	541	Harley	D H	8 Apr	1839	
40	Ibid	465	Harley		Nov	1838	
41	Ibid	480/1	Harley		29 Dec	1838	

42	Ibid		485	Harley				1838
43	Ibid		506	Harley			7 Feb	1839
44	Ibid		314	Ainsworth			28 Sep	1837
45	C C	Stave 3						
46	Ibid							
47	E J Bk 3	Ch 3	229					
48	*The Dickens Circle*, J. W. T. Ley							
49	P L Vol 1		492	Mitton			Jan	1839
50	Ibid		511	Mitton			22 Feb	1839
51	*The Dickens Originals*, E. Pugh				162/4			
52	P L Vol 1		358	Ainsworth		D H	25 Jan	1838
53	*Sketches of Young Couples*: 'The Nice Little Couple'							
54	*Phiz and Dickens*, Edgar Browne							
55	P L Vol 1		380	Talfourd			25 Feb	1838
56	Ibid		484	John Dickens			Dec	1838
57	Ibid		462	Hill		D H	29 Nov	1838
58	Ibid		489/90	Dr Quin			3 Jan	1839
59	Ibid		493	John Noble			21 Jan	1839
60	Ibid		493	Notes 1 and 2				
61	Ibid		514	Angus Fletcher			Feb	1839
62	Ibid		525/6	Beard		D H	13 Mar	1839
63	Ibid		546	Longman			Apr	1839
64	Ibid		545	Note 5				
65	Ibid		559 and Note 1	Miss Coutts			1 Jul	1839
66	Ibid		553	Note 1				
67	C C	Stave 3						
68	D	1905	205	Mrs F.			18 Jan	1847
69	D C	Ch 28						

Chapter 6 '*The Great Unpaid*'

1	D S	Ch 31						
2	Ibid	51						
3	Ibid	59						
4	*The Childhood and Youth of Dickens*, Stephen Langton							
5	D S	Ch 31						
6	P L Vol 1		144	T. C. Barrow		D H	31 Mar	1836
7	D C	Ch 11						
8	P L Vol 1		44	Mitton			21 Nov	1834
9	P P	Ch 40						
10	P L Vol 1		45	Mitton			21 Nov	1834
11	Ibid		48	Beard		D H	Dec	1834
12	Ibid		50	Mitton				1834
13	Ibid		454	Forster			15 Nov	1838
14	Ibid		47	Note 3				

15	Ibid		50	Beard	D H	16 Dec 1834
16	Ibid		51	Austin		20 Dec 1834
17	S		110			
18	Ibid					
19	E J Bk 3	Ch 5	255/6			
20	*Hundred Years*, Waugh and Straus		110			
21	S		110			
22	P L Vol 1		514	John Dickens		1838–9
23	Ibid		514	Forster		1 Mar 1839
24	Ibid		515	Forster		1 Mar 1839

Chapter 7 '*A jewel of a place*'

1	P L Vol 1		517	Mrs C. Dickens		5 Mar 1839
2	Ibid		518/20	Forster		15 Mar 1839
3	Ibid		521/3	Mrs C. Dickens		5 Mar 1839
4	Ibid		523/5	Mitton		6 Mar 1839
5	Ibid		526	Beard	D H	13 Mar 1839
6	Ibid		528	Dr F. P. B. Pickthorn		Mar 1839
7	Ibid		540	Mitton		7 Apr 1839
8	Ibid		527	Forster		Mar 1839
9	Ibid		560	Forster		11 Jul 1839
10	P L Vol 2		109	Forster		31 Jul 1840
11	S		110/1			
12	P L Vol 2		227	Mitton		9 Mar 1841
13	N L Vol 1		594	Mitton		17 Apr 1844
14	D C	Ch 54				
15	N L Vol 1		429	Mitton		4 Apr 1842
16	N L Vol 2		293	Forster		31 Mar 1851

Chapter 8 '*Bless his old gaiters*'

1	P P	Ch 39				
2	P L Vol 1		132	Chapman and Hall		18 Feb 1836
3	P P	Ch 34				
4	P L Vol 1		274	Forster		19 Jun 1837
5	Ibid		274	Forster		20 Jun 1837
6	P P	Ch 45				
7	P L Vol 1		280	Note 5 Forster		2 Jul 1837
8	Ibid		316	Note 4		
9	Ibid		322	Carey & Co		26 Oct 1837
10	Ibid		414	Leigh Hunt	D H	13 Jul 1838
11	Ibid		285	Bradbury & Evans	D H	20 Jul 1837
12	Ibid		287	C. Hicks	D H	20 Jul 1837
13	Ibid		289	G. Beadnell	D H	Jul 1837

14 P P   Ch 44
15 Ibid
16 Ibid   Ch 42
17 Ibid
18 P L Vol 1   161   Chapman and Hall D H   6 Aug 1836
19 Ibid   304   Forster   7 Sep 1837
20 F   109   Note 112
21 E J   102/3
22 P P   Ch 52
23 *Bingham's Law Report* 1827
24 P L Vol 1   340   Forster   11 Dec 1837
25 Ibid   341   Ainsworth   D H 11 Dec 1837
26 Ibid   368   Mrs H. Belcombe   8 Feb 1838
27 Ibid   315   Talfourd   1 Oct 1837
28 E J Vol 1   162
29 D Vol 33 1936/7   8

Chapter 9   *'The parish boy's progress'*

1 P L Vol 1   400   Note 3 and Agreement 658/9
2 Ibid   224   Bentley   18 Jan 1837
3 Ibid   453   Bentley   12 Nov 1838
4 Ibid   225   Bentley   20 Jan 1837
5 Ibid   234   Cruikshank   D H   8 Feb 1837
6 O T   Ch 3
7 P L Vol 1   472   Note 2
8 O T   Ch 2
9 *The Dickens World,* Humphrey House   94
10 P L Vol 1   328   Forster   3 Nov 1837
11 Ibid   439   Bentley   3 Oct 1838
12 Ibid   351   Talfourd   7 Jan 1838
13 Ibid   97   Note 1
14 Ibid   267   T. Haines   D H   3 Jun 1837
15 O T   Ch 11
16 Ibid   Ch 5
17 D   1910   62
18 E J Vol 2 Part 9 Ch 4 1010/1 Mrs E. Davis   1863
19 F Bk 2 Ch 3   111   Forster   1838
20 P L Vol 1   445   Bentley   27 Oct 1838
21 Ibid   353   Cruikshank   D H Mid Jan 1838
22 Ibid   440   Cruikshank   D H   6 Oct 1838
23 *Dickens and his Illustrators,* Kitton   16/17
24 Ibid
25 P L Vol 1   451   Note 1 Forster to Bentley   8 Nov 1839
26 F Bk 2 Ch 3   111   Forster   1838

27	N L Vol 3		702	Miss Mary Angela Dickens		27	Jan	1869
28	O T	Ch 21						
29	Ibid	Ch 48						
30	*Dickens House Guide*							
31	F Bk 2	Ch 2	108	Forster		9	Mar	1838
32	P L Vol 1		328	Forster		3	Nov	1837
33	Ibid		249	Bentley		20	Apr	1837
34	Ibid		538	Harley		1	Apr	1839
35	Ibid		525	Hill		13	Mar	1839
36	Ibid		429	Giles			Aug	1838
37	Ibid		452	Talfourd		10	Nov	1838
38	Ibid		454	Lytton		15	Nov	1838
39	Ibid		601	Ed. Chapman		14	Nov	1838
40	Ibid		350	Bentley			Jan	1838
41	Ibid		403 and Note 5 Lewes				Jun	1838
42	Ibid		437	Hicks		20	Sep	1838
43	O T Clarendon Edition, Prof. K. Tillotson xlvii							

Chapter 10 *'Here's richness!'*

1	P L Vol 1		668	Agreement (Brit Mus)		22	Sep	1838
2	Ibid		359	Ainsworth	D H	25	Jan	1838
3	Ibid		366	Mrs C. Dickens		1	Feb	1838
4	Dickens's Preface to first Cheap Edition of *Nicholas Nickleby*							
5	N N	Ch 39						
6	F Bk 2	Ch 2	107					
7	Ibid	Ch 4	124					
8	P L Vol 1		377	Forster			Feb	1838
9	Ibid		379	Chapman and Hall		22	Feb	1838
10	Ibid		381	Forster			Mar	1838
11	Ibid		385	Forster			Mar	1838
12	F Bk 2	Ch 2	109					
13	P L Vol 1		396	Forster		15	Apr	1838
14	Ibid		376	Cattermole			Feb	1838
15	Ibid		408	Hicks		29	Jun	1838
16	*The Englishman's Food*, J. C. Drummond 301							
17	N N	Ch 5						
18	F Bk 1	Ch 2	28					
19	N N	Ch 34						
20	Ibid	Ch 3						
21	*The Times*				D H	4	Jul	1829
22	N N	Ch 4						
23	P L Vol 1		411	Lord R. Grosvenor		9	Jul	1838
24	Ibid		456	Macready			Nov	1838
25	Ibid		457	Forster		20	Nov	1838

26 N N   Ch 15
27 D   Vol 55 No 328 89   'A Five-Year-Old Critic of *Nicholas*
                                Nickleby', W. J. Carlton
28 *Letters*, M. Dickens and G. Hogarth 18/19
29 P L Vol 1   467/8 R. H. Barham   Dec 1838
30 Ibid   481/3 Mrs S. C. Hall   D H 29 Dec 1838
31 N N   Ch 34
32 *The Dickens Originals*, E. Pugh
33 *With Dickens in Yorkshire*, T. P. Cooper 80/81
34 P L Vol 1   365   Mrs C. Dickens   1 Feb 1838
35 N N   Ch 8
36 P L Vol 1   493   John Noble   Jan 1839
37 F   Bk 2   Ch 4 125   Forster   1839
38 N N   Ch 49
39 *The Dickens Originals*, E. Pugh
40 *Letters*, M. Dickens and G. Hogarth 18 Mrs C. Dickens 1 Nov 1838
41 N N   Ch 24
42 P L Vol 1   225   Note 1
43 Ibid   553   Forster   7 Jun 1839
44 Ibid   556   Bradbury & Evans 18 Jun 1839
45 Ibid   561   Blanchard   Jul 1839
46 Ibid   513   Browne   D H   Feb 1839
47 Ibid   560   Browne   Jul 1839
48 N N   Ch 52
49 P L Vol 1   432   Note 5
50 Ibid   438   Note 2
51 Ibid   562   Note 1
52 *The Composition & Monthly Publication of Nicholas Nickleby*,
                                Dr Michael Slater
53 N N   Ch 16
54 P L Vol 1   598   Lady Holland   9 Nov 1839
55 Ibid   593   Macready   25 Oct 1839
56 Ibid   437   C. Hicks   20 Sep 1838
57 Ibid   558   Note 1
58 Ibid   577   Maclise   Summer 1839
59 Ibid   511   Forster   22 Feb 1839
60 Bibliography—Hatton & Cleaver (1933)
61 P L Vol 1   581   Forster   18 Sep 1839
62 Ibid   581   Forster   18 Sep 1839
63 N L Vol 1   194   Dickens's diary

Chapter 11 *Out of town*

 1 P L Vol 1   259   Beard   D H 17 May 1837
 2 N L Vol 1   481   Forster   5 Oct 1842

3	Ibid		510/1	Felton	2 Mar	1843
4	P P	Ch 46				
5	P L Vol 1		260/1	Ainsworth	17 and 21 May	1837
6	F Bk 2 Ch 1	92		Forster		1838
7	Ibid		93	Forster		1838
8	P L Vol 1		280	Forster	2 Jul	1837
9	Ibid		280	Note 4		
10	Ibid		280/1	Forster	2 Jul	1837
11	Ibid		303	E. S. Morgan	3 Sep	1837
12	F Bk 2 Ch 1	94/5		Forster	3 Sep	1837
13	R P 'Our English Watering Place'					
14	P L Vol 1		305	Bentley	13 Sep	1837
	Ibid			Mrs R. T. Thomson	14 Sep	1837
15	F Bk 2 Ch 1	95/6		Forster	3 Nov	1837
16	D S	Ch 8				
17	E J Part 3 Ch 3	214				
18	N N	Ch 5				
19	P L Vol 1		365	Mrs C. Dickens	1 Feb	1838
20	N N	Ch 42				
21	P L Vol 1		367	*Durham Advertiser*	Feb	1838
22	Ibid		406/7	Forster	23 Jun	1838
23	Ibid		406	Mrs A. Strickland	17 Jun	1838
24	N N	Ch 52				
25	P L Vol 1		410, 413	Bentley	3 and 10 Aug	1838
26	E J Part 3 Ch 3	221				
27	N L Vol 1		148	Dickens's diary		
28	Ibid		174	Mrs C. Dickens	1 Nov	1838
29	Ibid					
30	O C S	Ch 45				
31	N L Vol 1		149	Dickens's diary		
32	P L Vol 1		548	Forster	9 May	1839
33	Ibid		549	Hicks	D H 10 May	1839
34	Ibid		553	Macready	7 Jun	1839
35	Ibid		555	W. Behnes	11 Jun	1839
36	Ibid		556	Miss Mary Berry	Jun	1839
37	Richmond Public Library, letter to Maclise				28 Jun	1839
38	P L Vol 1		560/1	Blanchard	11 Jul	1839
39	Ibid		562	Forster	Jul	1839
40	Ibid		569	Mitton	26 Jul	1839
41	Ibid		567	Maclise	24 Jul	1839
42	Ibid		569	Fletcher	25 Jul	1839
43	Ibid		569	Mitton	26 Jul	1839
44	Ibid		571/2	Macready	26 Jul	1839
45	N N	Ch 50				

46	Ibid					
47	P L Vol 1	578	Forster	9	Sep	1839
48	N L Vol 3	120	M. A. and Kate Dickens	2	Sep	1859
49	N L Vol 2	114/5	Forster	10	Aug	1848
50	P L Vol 1	578/9	Forster	9	Sep	1839
51	Ibid	579	Fletcher	14	Sep	1839
52	Ibid	581/2	Forster	18	Sep	1839
53	Ibid					
54	Ibid	586	Thomas Ellar	27	Sep	1839

Chapter 12   *'These garish lights'*

1	O C S	Ch 39				
2	P L Vol 1	113	Hullah	29	Dec	1835
3	Ibid	150	Hullah	6	May	1836
4	Ibid	155	Macrone	20	Jul	1836
5	Ibid	162	Hullah	10	Aug	1836
6	Ibid	167	Hullah	22	Aug	1836
7	Ibid	175	Hullah	20	Sep	1836
8	Ibid	226	Harley	21	Jan	1837
9	D	1970	238 and 1971 97			
10	P L Vol 1	465	Note 4			
11	Ibid	245	Harley	D H 5	Apr	1837
12	Ibid	246	Harley	7	Apr	1837
13	*Letters*, M. Dickens and G. Hogarth 9 Harley Sat morning					
14	P L Vol 1	587/8	J. A. Overs	27	Sep	1839
15	Ibid	343	Harley	12	Dec	1837
16	Ibid	167	Note 3			
17	Ibid	314	Ainsworth	28	Sep	1837
18	Ibid	327	Forster	3	Nov	1837
19	Ibid	336	Note 1			
20	Ibid	348	Yates		Dec	1837
21	Ibid	355	Forster	16	Jan	1838
22	Ibid	386	Macready	13	Mar	1838
23	Ibid	409	Harley		Jun/Jul	1838
24	Ibid	440	Mrs Macready	4	Oct	1838
25	Ibid	444	Harley	24	Oct	1838
26	Ibid	506	Harley	7	Feb	1839
27	Ibid	448	Mrs Dickens	1	Nov	1838
28	Ibid	457	Forster	20	Nov	1838
29	Ibid	497	Cruikshank	26	Jan	1839
30	Ibid	520	Forster	5	Mar	1839
31	Ibid	523	Mrs Dickens	5	Mar	1839
32	Ibid	539	Macready		Apr	1839
33	Ibid	217	L. Blanchard	11	Jul	1839

34	Ibid	611	Macready	6 Dec 1839
35	Ibid	388/9	Yates	Mid Mar 1838
36	Ibid			
37	D 1947 'Early Dramas of *Oliver Twist*', M. Morley			
38	P L Vol 1	459/60	Forster	23 Nov 1838
39	Ibid	460	Note 1	
40	Ibid	464	Yates	29 Nov 1838
41	N N	Ch 48		

Afterword

1	P L Vol 1	596	Mrs Macready		1 Nov 1839
2	Ibid	597	Mitton		4 Nov 1839
3	Ibid	598	Forster		8 Nov 1839
4	Ibid	598	Forster		Nov 1839
5	Ibid	599/600	E. W. Banks	D H	11 Nov 1839

BIBLIOGRAPHY

Adrian, Arthur A., *Georgina Hogarth* (Oxford University Press, 1957).

Bingham's Law Report, 1827.

Browne, Edgar, *Phiz and Dickens* (James Nisbet & Co., London, 1913).

Butt, John and Tillotson, Kathleen, *Dickens at Work* (Methuen & Co., London, 1957).

Chancellor, Beresford, *The London of Charles Dickens* (Grant Richards Ltd., 1924).

Cooper, T. P., *With Dickens in Yorkshire* (Ben Johnson & Co., York, 1923).

Dexter, Walter, *The Letters of Charles Dickens* (Nonesuch Press, 1938).

Dickens, Charles, *The New Oxford Illustrated Dickens* (Oxford University Press).

Dickens, Charles, *Oliver Twist*, edited by Kathleen Tillotson (The Clarendon Press, Oxford, 1966).

The Dickens Fellowship, *The Dickensian*, 1905, 1910, 1936–7, 1947, 1955, 1959, (Dickens Fellowship, London).

Dickens, Mary and Hogarth, Georgina, *The Letters of Charles Dickens* (Macmillan, London, 1893).

Drummond, J. C., *The Englishman's Food* (Jonathan Cape Ltd., London, 1939).

Fielding, K. J., *The Speeches of Charles Dickens* (Oxford University Press, 1960).

Forster, John, *The Life of Charles Dickens*, annotated by J. W. T. Ley (Cecil Palmer, 1928).

Hatton, T. and Cleaver, A. H., *Bibliography of the Works of Charles Dickens* (Chapman and Hall, 1933).

House, Humphrey, *The Dickens World* (Oxford University Press, 1941).

House, Madeline and Storey, Graham, *The Letters of Charles Dickens* (Pilgrim Edition, The Clarendon Press, 1965, 1969).

Johnson, Edgar, *Charles Dickens: His Tragedy and Triumph* (Simon & Schuster, New York, 1952).

Kitton, F. C., *Dickens and his Illustrators* (George Redway, London, 1899).

Langton, Stephen, *The Childhood and Youth of Dickens* (Hutchinson & Co. Ltd., 1891).

Ley, J. W. T., *The Dickens Circle* (E. P. Dutton & Co., New York, 1919).

Palmer, Arnold, *Moveable Feasts* (Oxford University Press, 1952).

Pugh, Edwin, *The Dickens Originals* (T. N. Foulis, London, 1912).

Slater, Michael, *Composition and Monthly Publication of Nicholas Nickleby* (The Scholar Press, 1973).

Straus, Ralph, *A Portrait of Dickens* (J. M. Dent & Sons Ltd., London, 1928).

Waugh, A., *A Hundred Years of Publishing* (Chapman and Hall, 1930).

INDEX